S·I·M·P·L·I·C·I·T·Y

These are only hints and guesses,
Hints followed by guesses;
And the rest is prayer, observance, discipline,
Thought and action.
The hint half guessed, the gift half understood,
Is Incarnation.

—*"The Dry Salvages," T. S. Eliot*

O Lord, don't ever let us move into stone houses.

—*A poor man in Nairobi*

S·I·M·P·L·I·C·I·T·Y

THE ART OF LIVING

Richard Rohr

Translated by Peter Heinegg

CROSSROAD • NEW YORK

1991

The Crossroad Publishing Company
370 Lexington Avenue, New York, NY 10017

Originally published under the title
Von der Freiheit loszulassen — Letting Go
translated and introduced by Andreas Ebert
© Claudius Verlag Munich 1990
English translation copyright © 1991
by The Crossroad Publishing Company

Printed in the United States of America
Typesetting output: TEXSource, Houston

Library of Congress Cataloging-in-Publication Data

Rohr, Richard.
    [Von der Freiheit loszulassen. English]
    Simplicity : the art of living / Richard Rohr ; translated by
Peter Heinegg.
    p. cm.
    Translation of: Von der Freiheit loszulassen, lectures delivered
in Germany and Switzerland, March 1990.
    ISBN 0-8245-1133-6
    1. Christian life—1960– 2. Church and the world. I. Title.
BV4501.2.R655 1991
252′.02—dc20   91-19044
                                               CIP

*For the little ones everywhere,
who hold before the world the secrets
of the ever-coming Christ.*

*For the family, friars, and friends
who gave me the eyes and heart
to recognize their simple secret.*

Contents

Foreword

I N MARCH 1990 after a long absence Richard Rohr returned again to the German-speaking world. In this book we have documented some of the talks and sermons he gave in Basel, Dresden, Nuremberg, Giessen, and Darmstadt. His subjects have remained the same as ever — and yet there are new tones here. Richard Rohr is discovering more and more the contemplative side of faith, the process of becoming empty and letting go, as Meister Eckhart and the German mystics in particular preached and practiced it. Once again we are taken along on an exciting journey, once again we are challenged not only to rethink things, but to live in a new and different way.

The lectures and conversations were translated sentence for sentence into German and recorded on tape. The translator at the talks in Basel was Harald Walach; at the afternoon conversation in Basel it was Frank S. Lorenz; at all the meetings in Germany it was Andreas Ebert. Constanze Keutler-Hagl put together the first version of the text, working from the tapes. Marion Küstenmacher edited these transcriptions, and Andreas Ebert took over the final editing. For the book version repetitions were removed unless that disturbed the flow of ideas. On the other hand we have kept some of the spontaneous unevenness of impromptu talk to document as much of the original atmosphere as possible.

Two Voices from Switzerland

Pastor Felix Felix, in *Rundbrief der Diakonischen Gemeinschaft,* Friedensgasse, Basel, March 1990, pp. 12–14:

It was said of Jesus that he spoke with authority and not like the doctors of the law. For he taught from his soul, from his life and his experience, from what he had learned and understood in his meetings with children, women, and men, with himself and the "devil," but also with his Father in heaven.

When you meet somebody who also teaches "with authority," who has something to say, who senses what his audience's current concerns are because they concern himself, then you get the feeling that you already knew what you just heard: "Actually there was nothing new. I've felt that before too; it's just that I couldn't put it into words before." We don't feel stupid — as opposed to being some heavy-duty genius — but like people who already know by ourselves, who have been encouraged to rely on ourselves, to listen to ourselves, and to trust better what we hear, sense, and guess there. For we all bear within us the real teacher and master. Jesus calls him the Holy Spirit, who will lead us to all truth. This doesn't mean that we don't need one another any more, but that we can stop looking for the master and hanging on the lips of a teacher. That may still be necessary when we're children, but mature persons heed the teacher in their hearts.

Nevertheless teachers have been given to us who can strengthen us with their words and enable us to hear with our outer ears what the reality in which we live and the Holy Spirit too have long wanted to teach us. That's why it was valuable to meet Richard Rohr. His talks, which were very well attended in spite of Mardi Gras, have given courage and hope to many people. Someone said to me: "This time I didn't leave with the feeling, 'Now you've got to do this and that too, and then it'll be good.' I wasn't driven on to more achievement, but to more trust: Let go, trust in God, trust in life, and what it teaches you."

Rohr doesn't teach passivity but active trust, action and contemplation, commitment in the world, and the ability to let go in God.... One beautiful experience for me was that much of what has become important for me in the last few years and what for some people is still tarred with the brush of liberation theology, feminism, New Age, or worse — I found all this treated by Rohr the Franciscan as old, simple, joyful Franciscan theology — if we may label it theology at all. Perhaps it's better to call it the simple joy in God, in Jesus Christ, in creation and creatures that became perceptible in the spirit of Brother Francis. This wasn't the *Zeitgeist* speaking, but the spirit of Jesus and the Sermon on the Mount.

Beat Rüegger, in *Reformiertes Forum* 12
(March 23, 1990): 19:

I'm still elated — but not by the Mardi Gras. I like that here in Basel too, but the reason lies elsewhere: On two succeeding evenings there was a talk in our church. Or rather, there was a meeting with a person who in the literal, original sense is filled with Gospel "enthusiasm." Richard Rohr, the Franciscan priest and author, also guided his audience to risk taking a look at the Church that could be but isn't (yet).

What kept impressing me again and again and what I have found in the Church and not just in this man is this: It's possible, without excuses and digressions, to point out and admit that to us Western Christians bourgeois con-

sumer culture is much closer than the Reign of God. So
in this sense our present-day Christianity is frighteningly
infected by the viruses of "wealth," "security," and "national egoism." But on the other hand and at the same time
it is possible despite everything to remain bound in love to
this Church and its tradition. This sort of attitude is often
scarcely understood. Anyone who relentlessly unmasks the
real existing situation is easily labeled a complainer, a be-
fouler of his own nest. But it's precisely the ones that poke
a critical nose into things who have kept alive a special love
for their Church or the country they live in. They butt in
precisely because it's important to them that their Church
or country doesn't go off on any old path. I hope we learn to
give more of a welcome to these voices of unpleasant med-
dling, especially in the Church. They might be prophetic
voices. During his talk Richard Rohr paraphrased a saying
of Augustine, that "many belong to the Church who don't
belong to God, but many belong to God who don't belong
to the Church."

As if this saying had needed an illustration, the following episode occurred: A man, who didn't exactly cor-
respond to our notion of the average churchgoer, quite
obviously not pampered by life, with an old-fashioned artificial leg and wearing an unconventional suit, walked
cautiously with his large dog through the center aisle of the
church, past the astonished public, silently placed a burning candle in front of the pulpit, and then quietly sat down
along the side aisle. I wish there was more such openness,
such natural ease in church. The interest of the audience
proved there might be a chance of it there. The church
was nearly full both times. At Mardi Gras in Basel that says
something.

                                                    ANDREAS EBERT

Preface

THE MYTHS OF MODERNISM are dying all around us. Our sophistication and complexity are self-destructing. For several hundred years we were convinced in the West that progress, human reason, and higher technology would resolve the human dilemma. They clearly have not. Without denying the gifts of mind and science, we now doubt their messianic promise. More analysis is not necessarily more wisdom, and more options are not necessarily freedom. The accumulation of things is not likely to bring more happiness, and time saved is rarely used for contemplation.

Progress has too often been at the expense of the earth, and human reason has too easily legitimated war, greed, and the pursuit of a private agenda, while technology pays those who serve it, especially the moguls of militarism and medicine. Our philosophy of progress has led us to trust in our own limitlessness and in our future more than in the quality and the mystery of the *now*. Religion at its best is always concerned about the depth and breadth and wonder of things. In this sense we have become an impatient and irreligious people. The paschal mystery, the yin and yang of all reality, is outshouted by the quite recent and unproven slogan: "we can have it all!"

T. S. Eliot struggles with this chosen blindness in his fourth quartet, "Little Gidding":

> Not known, because not looked for
> But heard, half-heard, in the stillness
> Between two waves of the sea.
> Quick now, here, now, always —
> A condition of complete simplicity
> (Costing not less than everything)

The cost, of course, is the problem. The almost impossible task of the Church is to offer both the promise
and the price — simultaneously. Promise without price
becomes sweet sentimentality; price without promise becomes shame, burden, and grief. We have enough of both.
But who will point us back to the "condition of complete
simplicity"? And who wants to go? I do believe there is a
divine therapy both for the individual and for the Church.
It is the radical contemplative stance. Aldous Huxley rightly
called it "the perennial philosophy." It is the return to
simplicity that comes from lots of good looking and good
listening. I will go so far as to say, "There is no other way."
But the cost is not less than everything:

> To come to the pleasure you have not
> you must go by a way in which you enjoy not.
> To come to the knowledge you have not
> you must go by a way in which you know not.
> To come to the possession you have not
> you must go by a way in which you possess not.
> To come to be what you are not
> you must go by a way in which you are not.
>
> St. John of the Cross, I, 13, #10
> *The Ascent of Mt. Carmel*

Now that is lost wisdom, yet it recurs in every age and
in every religion. But reason would never lead us there,

and certainly not a philosophy of progress, efficiency, or "self-actualization." It is called "revelation." It is waited for, needed, desired, and received as wondrous grace. It is never logically concluded. That's why Jesus says that it is only *faith* that "saves."

My loss of innocence has been slow in coming. I now see that it is just as hard for the Church to believe as it is for the individual. I am really not sure which comes first, but right now they are both pointing accusing fingers at one another to avoid their own treacherous journey. I know that the Church body cannot ask of its members what it has not exemplified; and the members cannot ask of the Body what they will not risk themselves. Who goes first? The divine alchemy of history never tells us for sure. Did More and Newman form the English church or did the English church form them? I don't suppose that we need to know. "Not to us, O God, not to us, but to your name give the glory" (Psalm 115:1).

And same for the blame. The amorphous guilt must go somewhere. We used to accuse ourselves mercilessly, and now we do the same to parents, institutions, or history itself. There must be a victim and a victimizer. But why? What does it help? Maybe that is why Jesus became the cosmic victim and refused to condemn the victimizers: "They know not what they do" (Luke 23:34).

We are ready and oh so in need of mercy. The painful mystery of things, the injustice of it all, the mixed blessing, just *is*. Nothing is gained by accusing or avoiding, except a false sense of control. History is ours and we are history. All of it. The Church might best be described as the place where that can honestly happen, where *all* of history can be carried, and carried toward redemption. To isolate any part, or to isolate the whole in favor of a part, is to maim and deface the Body of Christ. It is also to refuse our part in the great human experiment.

To believe in the ongoing mystery of the Church is to be willing to work with history, its level of consciousness, its issues, at my chronological moment on this planet. I will not refuse my place in the great chain of Being; I will live now "for better for worse, for richer for poorer, till death do us part." That is our concrete marriage to Christ. And what other Christ can we meet? What other Christ (or Church?) did we expect? What pagan hubris allows us to think that we can jump ahead or stubbornly hide in the past?

But I must also admit that I have never found it harder to believe in the Church. God's redemption of history seems so utterly slow and ineffective, and even impeded by the Church politic. Is one step forward and three backward the only way to proceed? Somebody is very patient, certainly more than I. Bishops sanctimoniously proclaim their pro-life stance and calmly bless the murder of 150,000 Iraqis by the U.S. government. They claim to be certain about God's will in regard to birth control, married priests, women priests, and all manner of sexual conduct (about which Jesus says little or nothing) and yet live in comfortable doubt about God's will in regard to war, riches, and non-violence (about which Jesus is absolutely clear). This is magisterium? Give me a break! The pope appoints echo-chamber bishops throughout the world, controls the minutiae of a universal, multi-cultural church, and yet still hopes to speak with authority about Providence, social justice, and trust in God. It just doesn't sell anymore. Faith saves, control controls and not much more.

But we are no better. Liberals consider obedience and surrender an affront to their freedom and "wholeness." Conservatives make freedom a bad word, while living on full bended knee before the free market and the supposed freedom of America. Patriarchs live in naive ignorance of their privileged state, while ideological feminists read all of human history through one self-serving paradigm. Lay boards and communities show all of the triumphalism and ego-tripping that the clergy once mastered. How is anyone supposed to see the glorious face of Christ in the midst of such smallness and disbelief? Why would anyone accept evangelization from a people so divided and with such little good news?

But "to whom else shall we go?" (John 6:68). Individualism leads to eccentricity and arrogance, New Agers finally become articulate narcissists, and cultural gadflies move with every trendy breeze. I have worked with too many Native Americans to buy the pseudo-Indian spirituality that floats around New Mexico, and I appreciate the creation spirituality of my Franciscan tradition too much to think that it was just discovered in California. Even the much needed Twelve Step programs have become their own kind of addiction and avoidance of the "painful mystery of things." Let's face it, there is no support group, therapy, theology, or mystic ceremony that is going to take all the pain away.

Even if I had a great gift for writing, this book wouldn't take the mystery away either. But I believe in the truth of the basic Gospel more than ever, and so I am compelled to preach and teach. Others tape and transcribe, and this book is a result. I hope it will resolve a few contemporary obstacles so that the Gospel can again be gospel, good news *for all the peoples* (Mark 11:17). I hope it will not delay you in your passage through that messy gap between the two naivetés: the first is dangerous simplicity, uncritical and unconnected; the second naiveté is blessed simplicity, calm, knowing, patient, self-forgetful because all has been remembered. It is these second simpletons who reinvent the Gospel in every age.

I write this small preface while recovering from un-expected surgery for malignant melanoma. Two weeks ago I thought my life on this earth was over, and I was asking God "why?" I could not deny that I have had a most wonderful life: rich, varied, "full measure, pressed down, shaken together, running over, and poured into my lap" (Luke 6:38). Just when I thought I had said yes, Someone said no, and for now I live again. Is there more room in my lap? Is there room in God's? I'll bet there is. There is always enough room for simplicity.

FR. RICHARD ROHR, O.F.M.
Center for Action and Contemplation
Albuquerque, New Mexico
June 1991

1   God the Father— God the Mother?

WHENEVER WE DISCUSS THIS SUBJECT IN AMERICA, there's always a lot of controversy and misunderstanding. Maybe that says something about how much time we need to let God be free. We often say that it's the role of the prophet to keep people free for God. But at the same time it's the responsibility of the prophet to keep God free for people.

I'd like to begin with something that looks like a cliché: with the First Commandment. It says that we're not supposed to make any images of God nor to worship them. We've never taken the First Commandment seriously. God created human beings after God's own image, and we've returned the compliment, so to speak, creating God after our image. Thus God or the gods were, as a rule, turned into a mirror image and projection of our own selves. In the end we produced what was mostly a kind of tribal god. In America God looks like Uncle Sam or Santa Claus. In any case he's a white Anglo-Saxon. I just spent nine days in England, where God looks like the British Empire. A Swiss God, perhaps, resembles a banker or a psychologist.

Normally we find it very, very difficult to let God really

A talk given in the Church of St. Matthew, Basel, March 7, 1990.

be God, a God who's greater than our culture and our projections. In patriarchal Europe we prefer to see God as a man. And yet it says right there in Genesis: "God created humankind in God's own image; male and female God created them" (Gen. 1:27). That says point blank that God cannot be masculine. And yet we seem to need still more proof.

Despite all our theology, when this sort of question arises the dominant culture normally carries the day. Or rather what ultimately prevails is the human ego. We always seem to find a way to keep things firmly in our grasp. And so we've created "God" to go on playing our game: a God who fits into our system. A God who stands outside our system and calls to us is something we can't endure. Thus, for example, we've continually needed a God who likes to play war just as much as we do. We've needed a domineering God, because we ourselves like to dominate. And since we're so fixated on this, we've almost completely forgotten and ignored what Jesus told us about God and the nature of God.

At first glance the First Commandment deals only with carved or handmade likenesses of God. But it refers above all to those images of God that we assemble in our heads and keep there. The great figures of faith that I know are always letting go of their momentary, self-related images of God. But that calls for a high degree of distance from oneself. Perhaps that's why faith is so rare and religion so widespread: Because religion is very often a means to maintain our comfortable image of God, even when it's pathological and destructive. We feel better with what we know, even when it does us in.

But faith always invites us to a new place that we're not quite familiar with. Thus we can see in the Book of Exodus how the Israelites preferred to go back to slavery in Egypt rather than be led into the wilderness, where they didn't have God in the palm of their hands. When we grow, our image of God and our self-image normally move forward on parallel tracks. And if one of the two breaks down, the other has to come apart too. We stick to both of them, and both stick together. Every crisis of faith implies that one or the other side is cracking up. If you really grow in faith, then in my opinion this process ought to take place at least every two or three years. This is the darkness of faith: when you've had to drop the old for a time but haven't yet found the new. It's the terrible space in between, where nobody wants to live. And we want to retreat to a spot where I know who I am and who God is — even when our self-image and our image of God destroy one another, which often happens.

The journey of faith demands that we let go of our image of God and our image of ourselves. But we can't do that in our head or on our own; it's done *to* us. The only thing we have to do is live, but live openly and honestly and let the truth of the world get to us. We're not converted in our heads or by sermons from the pastor: We're converted by circumstances — if we really let the circumstances get to us. And when you let reality get to you, then it doesn't take very long. When you really let God get to you, then the Santa Claus image of God doesn't work very long. When you really let God get to you, the masculine image of God doesn't last very long either.

Since we need a license to hurl thunderbolts, we've created a Zeus-god who hurls them too. But as soon as we head to a place where we discover something tender and soft, the Zeus-image of God no longer works. As soon as we go on an inner journey and discover a place full of compassion, broad and vast, the Zeus-image of God doesn't work any more. Jesus went into the wilderness for forty days (Matt. 4:2), where he got rid of his images. He was emptied. And that's the real meaning of fasting: to be emptied of your own images. Only when Jesus was emptied of his self-image could the Father give him a new image and call him "dear son." And we can't deny that Jesus felt good about calling his God "father."

Presumably that also had something to do with his patriarchal culture, even if he did dare to called his God "abba," the word little boys used, like "papa" or "daddy" with us. It probably also says a lot about his human father, Joseph, and about his relationship with him. But we see clearly in Jesus' parables and metaphors that he usually describes his father-God in images we would call feminine. This is especially true of the story of the prodigal son (Luke 15:11–32) and when he says that God would gladly be a hen and take us under his wings like little chicks (Matt. 23:27).

One of the main features of my work in America is retreats and counselling for priests. And although these men know a great deal about theology, I've found to my surprise that their image of God is 90 percent a mixture of the image of their own mothers and fathers. And for some reason they themselves are always amazed when they discover this. If their mother was harshly critical, so is their God. If their father was distant and cold, then their God is distant and cold. I would like to encourage you to check and see to what extent this applies to your life as well.

Once again, we have to break through the images to find the God who really is God. I promise you there's nothing you need to be afraid of here. But you have no reason to believe that until you take the journey yourself. People who really pray always know that. People who empty themselves in the wilderness always meet a God who is greater than they would have dared to hope. The American Trappist monk Thomas Merton, a man who had a great deal of influence on me, describes this experience as "mercy, within mercy, within mercy." There's always a lot of anxiety and insecurity involved in letting go of your current images of yourselves and your images of God. Only God can lead you, and the only thing you can do is let go. The spiritualities of all great world religions teach us letting go: how to step aside.

I'm convinced that we have, especially in the northern European countries, transformed the Gospel into self-control. On the other hand I'm convinced that the Gospel itself is about self-surrender. But self-control is a masculine way of thinking. And self-surrender is perhaps rather a feminine form of thinking. We haven't allowed God to teach us to surrender.

The groups growing the fastest in America nowadays are called Twelve Step programs. They were created fifty years ago by a man named Bill Wilson, when he founded Alcoholics Anonymous. If they go on growing as they have till now, someday there will be four such groups for every one Church. These groups talk about self-surrender, but the Church talks about self-control. Also they don't gather in rectangular churches with a pulpit in the middle, which normally enthrones the left hemisphere of the brain, the more masculine kind of thinking. They gather in a circle, and they share their pain with one another. No therapist comes in to psychoanalyze them, and no charismatic comes in to pray over them. It's nothing but purely and simply the mystery of the naked body of Christ, when people share their trust and their pain.

When people get together in solidarity and unity, not out

of power but out of powerlessness, then Christ is in their midst. And I find, if I'm honest, a lot more healing in these simple groups than in most of our churches. I also have a sense of it as a much more feminine image of the Church with a much more feminine image of God: God as a healer, as a person who participates and doesn't just think.

Like many other people I've continually wondered why Jesus came to us as a man and why he chose twelve men. I have only my interpretation for this and no proof that it's right. But I think that if Jesus had come as a woman, and had this woman been forgiving and compassionate, and had she taught non-violence, we wouldn't have experienced that as revelation. "Oh, well, a typical woman," we would have said. But the fact that a man in a patriarchal society took on these qualities that we call "feminine" was a breakthrough in revelation. So he spent three years teaching twelve men how to do things differently — and they almost never caught on. And for two thousand years the men in the Church have never caught on. Because we men wanted a God of domination. We've needed a God who would allow the Germans to kill the French and the French to kill the English. A feminine God wouldn't have gotten the job done. The Sermon on the Mount went down the drain. In the men's Church there is no room for turning the other cheek and forgiving one's enemies.

Ever since the Sermon on the Mount the Gospel and Western civilization have been on a collision course. But the collision course turned into a one-way street. And the winner wasn't Jesus; the winner was Western civilization. We've taken Jesus over and placed a crown on his head, not a crown of thorns, but a royal crown, which he expressly rejected. But we need kings to keep England, France, and all the other countries in line.

So he taught his twelve apostles how it could be done differently. We see, for example, in the Gospel of Mark how he tells his disciples three times: We must die, we must lose, we must be powerless. And each time they either don't get it or they change the subject. And the first one not to catch on is Peter, the so-called Prince of the Apostles. By the way, this is also the only time Jesus calls one of his beloved disciples a "devil" (Mark 8:33). He's saying: "You haven't understood at all what I'm after."

Until the end of Mark's Gospel it's always the men who don't understand what it's all about and who never get what Jesus is talking about. The women, on the other hand, always understand. And the first witness to the resurrection is not a man, but a prostitute, Mary Magdalen. For the Church's first thousand years she was called an apostle. This can now be proven from liturgical texts. She was even called the "apostle to the apostles." The fact that she *was* just that is clear from all four Gospels.

What then does the Gospel say? It predicts what really happened later: that we would have a hard time with a feminine God, with a God of forgiveness, a God of sympathy, a God of contact. Where did Jesus learn to wash the feet of his apostles (John 13:5)? In the previous chapter his own feet are washed by a woman, Mary (12:3)! This is no theology located in the head, but a theology that feels at ease in the body.

By now I've had the wonderful experience of preaching in almost all the parts of the world. And it's becoming increasingly clear to me that different parts of the world feel comfortable in different parts of the body. The continent of Europe undoubtedly feels most at ease in the head, while the Africans, for example, perhaps feel most at ease in their bodies without all the shame that most of us sense when we look at our body. I believe that if we had a more feminine face of God, we wouldn't have the terrible problems with authority and sexuality we struggle with in our Church and culture.

In the Middle Ages we tried to even out this imbalance through the image of Mary. We Catholics have often exaggerated this. It may have been bad theology to treat Mary as if she were God, but it was very good and even necessary psychology. We needed a feminine face for God. From the eleventh to the thirteenth centuries most of the churches in Europe were called "Notre Dame" or "Frauenkirche." It was as if the whole soul were longing for a God as tender and gentle as she was.

I remember a time when I was a little boy in Kansas. Our priests and nuns, who came from Ireland, tried to encourage us little Catholics to pray the rosary. They said: "When you get to heaven, St. Peter will be standing there at the gate. Of course, he's got the key, but he's a man. And you can peek through the gate, and there you see Jesus, but he's a man too. And then you look past Jesus, and there sits the old man on the throne." But, these good Irish sisters said, "There's a secret entrance way" — this will sound super-Catholic nowadays and extremely heretical — "Go to the back entrance to heaven!" They said: "If you're a good boy, and you've prayed your rosary, Mary will be at the back window, and the rosary will hang down and pull you up into heaven."

Horrible theology — but a good idea, once you understand it. Because most people grew up with conditional love from their father and unconditional love from their mother. Actually that wasn't true for me: I have a good German-born mother, who was in charge of discipline in our family and never let us get away with anything. My father, on the other hand, was very soft. He may also be the reason I've written books on masculine spirituality and why I feel very comfortable with the image of God as a father. As you can see, what's at stake here is not so much theology as the question: How does God come to each one of us? Sometimes God must come as a friend and another time as a lover; another time it may be good if God comes as a father. But if you continue on your spiritual journey, I promise you that some time God will reveal himself in feminine form: himself as herself. And for some of us that may be the first time that we fall in love with God.

Many people, I find, don't love God at all — maybe even most people, even very many religious people. To my surprise I've discovered that many religious men and women even hate God. Naturally they can't admit that to themselves. How many people are afraid of God, how many experience God as cold and absent, how many people have a sense of God as someone who might toy with them or undercut them. They have nothing to be afraid of. The only thing we can lose is that false image that we don't need. That image of ourselves that's always too small and that image of God that's always too small too. You don't have to do anything at all when you leave here. Just ask God to teach you to let go.

In the end I come back to Mary. The image of Mary is so perfect because she seems to have the ability to make herself empty. Her womb was empty. She was ready to let go of what her own theology told her about God. No monotheistic Jewish girl at that time could ever have been prepared for the incarnation. God is perfectly transcendent and beyond everything. And if she believed the rabbis' teaching that God comes in words, in the Torah and in the Commandments, then nothing prepared her for believing that God could become flesh and a body.

The whole thing had nothing to do with theology. It was rather about vulnerability, about letting go, about emptiness, about self-surrender — and none of all that is in the head. It was a woman who said yes, so that Jesus could come into the world. And the more the Church gets out of its head and into its feminine soul, the more, I believe, it will become able to conceive Christ and carry him to term for the world. Not a Christ we could fight over as Catholics or Protestants, as liberals or conservatives, but simply a Christ you can meet, a Christ you can stumble on, a Christ who won't let people "know" him, only love him.

QUESTIONS and ANSWERS

Q. *Is the Basel Mardi Gras that we're celebrating just now another kind of self-surrender?*

A. I'm very impressed by the way Mardi Gras is celebrated here. For those of you who know the Enneagram: Switzerland is a ONE country, and what happens at Mardi Gras on the streets here is SEVEN energy. That's exactly the consolation point that ONEs have to find: To come to rest and integration, ONEs have to integrate SEVEN within themselves. So in their Mardi Gras tradition the Swiss show they have a natural sense for what does them good.

Q. *Two men were canonized in Rome at practically the same time: Philip Neri, "God's jester" with his "Oratory," and Ignatius Loyola. Which of the two do you think is closer to us today?*

A. I don't want to be anti-Jesuit just because I'm a Franciscan. But to echo the Enneagram (and this is just one way of stating the case), Ignatius is a ONE and speaks a rather moralistic, perfectionist language. I'm not sure whether we need any more of that, even if we have Ignatius to thank for some wonderful instruments for the discernment of spirits. I suspect that your woman's intuition is right, that Philip Neri's playfulness and heart-centeredness might be better for many of us. We've made redemption into very serious business, and we may have forgotten how to play before the Lord. Our mothers perhaps let us play in front of them, while our fathers taught us to exert ourselves and be good boys. Philip Neri probably had a good mother, and maybe a very free father.

Q. *I see how the masculine predominates in the language of our Church, even in the Bible. Do you have some helpful hints for a different kind of terminology?*

A. That's a gigantic problem right now. You're perfectly right: The liturgical texts are almost completely patriarchal, and they perpetuate this narrow image of God. I've heard that this is even more difficult in German than in other languages. In the U.S. many books have been rewritten by nuns in a new, non-sexist, and inclusive language. In our community we've placed great value on that. Many people think it's unimportant, but language is very important because it establishes the categories that we interpret our experience with. I'd like to encourage you to hold on to the words that I call "sexually charged" (there's lots of power in them). For example, the words "father" or "mother" are sexually charged, whereas the word "parent" is neutral and flat. If we said, "my parent," there would be no energy behind it. In English we try to avoid the word "men" when we're talking about people. The subject deserves a more detailed treatment, but for now these little hints may do.

Q. *Do you have any tips for us so we can change the forms in which we're still moving in the churches and which prevent us from expressing and realizing what you've just said?*

A. That's a question for a weekend workshop. You're completely right: The structures are unequivocally patriarchal. In Catholicism the structure is patriarchal; in Protestantism the thought models are very masculine: the pulpit in the center. Obviously a kind of balance could be struck if the rational and the non-rational, the left and the right halves of the brain, were given equal rights: an altar and a pulpit in the center of a circle. That's also why I brought up the image of the Twelve Step program, because it's an image of the "Church from below." I believe that, regardless of what denomination we're from, we'll make progress only by doing what we have to do. But don't leave the Church and don't let yourselves be thrown out either. What we have to do has to be done in a creative tension with history and with our ancestors. That's the only way that we'll finally influence history.

In many ways the structures of the Church represent the point where history finds itself just now. And you belong to the first generation of the Church that has broken through to this insight with great clarity, though we have to say that in the course of history many individuals have already done that too — but as individuals. I like to say that as a Church we've grown a year per century, as far as our readiness for Christ goes. That means that by now we're almost twenty years old. We're now beginning to pose adult questions to the Bible.

Many questions of the Reformation were asked by male clerics fighting with other male clerics. They were questions for teenagers: Who's right? Who has the power? Now we're twenty years old, young adults. Now we're ready to learn how to meet one another and love one another. As you do that, the history of the Church unfolds. But don't drop tradition: It's mothered us and fathered us, till we got to the point where we are now. We carry its burden, but we also carry its freedom. Despite all our burdens, this question of women's insight is arising above all on the soil of Western Christianity.

Q. *Shouldn't we just leave theology aside so we can move on to spirituality? We get stuck with the theology in our heads.*

A. We use the concept of the right and left half of the brain, which didn't become a fairly clear principle until 1981. Now there are studies about where the individual nations stand along a continuum between the right and left hemispheres of the brain. German-speaking people have the strongest tendency to left-brain thinking in the world. That's not meant as an insult: my parents speak German too.

The question you've asked is very important. Still I don't want to play down how important good theology is. If I hadn't received good theology, I wouldn't have the authority to stand here and say all this. But at the same time I'd like to stress how important spirituality is above everything else. And once again I'd like to say what I already said in the beginning, that religion is one of the surest ways to avoid faith. Religion is one of the surest methods to

avoid God. That was shown to us in the New Testament by
the murderers of Jesus. It was the priests and theologians
who killed Jesus. And the ones who accepted him were the
lepers, the drunkards, and the prostitutes. In liberation theology this is called the "preferential option for the poor."
Truth isn't where we suppose. As Jesus says: "Be prepared
for the surprise that the first will be last, and the last will
be first " (Matt. 19:30).

Q. *Is the Adversary, the devil, merely a projection, or do you
think that there's also a real power of evil here?*

A. As a student I put exactly the same question to my professor. And he answered that it would really be very hard
simply to shove aside the whole Bible, all of tradition, and
all world religions, which generally seem to assume that
there are personal evil spirits in the world. Many Indians
in New Mexico, where I live, have no doubt at all that
the devil exists. And they even carry out exorcisms over
the areas where we build atomic weapons. In our cerebral theology we're not so sure that there is a devil. But
we go out and build the atom bombs. There are two ex-
tremes: either to take the devil seriously, or simply deny
his existence. Personally I've had too many experiences to
simply deny the existence of a personal evil presence in
the world.

Tradition has said there are three sources of evil: first,
the world or the "system," as I call it, institutional evil,
structural sin — until now we've paid little attention to
this. Second, is the flesh, but by that we don't mean sex,
even if most people think so: We mean the personalized
lie, the personalized wound, the personalized rage that I
carry around with me in my body. The third source of evil

is the devil. Frankly I think we should approach evil in this order: first the world, then the flesh, and finally the devil.

Q. *How could Jesus in good conscience give the twelve apostles the order to evangelize when they were thorough failures and hadn't understood anything until that point? And after Pentecost why didn't the feminine Holy Spirit manage to make something sensible out of these men even then?*

A. Naturally I'm not wise enough to see through history, especially now that the facts have been established. But I think all this shows the power of the first source of evil, the world: We are much more caught up in social prejudices than we ever noticed: racism, sexism, classism. And the only lesson I can draw from this is that whoever this God is, God is very patient. It's apparently God's wish that the truth *unfold in us,* and that's the great risk of the Incarnation. It seems as though God wanted neither to believe in control nor to force the truth upon us. But if we can believe Jesus, then God comes to us in powerlessness and vulnerability. God has even allowed us to commit many terrible mistakes with the Gospel. God has enough authority and power to wait. In the language of masculine spirituality I call that "healthy male energy." In this sense God is actually male, although in history the virtue of patience was shown much more often by women.

Q. *You have described patience and devotion and love as typically feminine qualities, in contrast to the cerebral thinking of the male. Isn't there a danger here that women in society will remain bound to this role forever? Hasn't the veneration of Mary become an instrument of patriarchal theology in just*

*that way? Perhaps women don't want to stay at the back door,
smuggling people in, but to stand in front alongside Peter, key
in hand?*

A. That's why I tried to say that some qualities are *possibly* "feminine," and can be equally held by women or by
men. It's very dangerous to call certain qualities masculine
or feminine. Even if it's true, of course, that the culture has
defined a certain bundle of qualities as masculine and rewarded them in men, and conversely with other qualities
in women. The goal is for all of us to become "wild men"
and "wild women." And then we'll both have our journey
behind us, and we can meet in the end as possessors of
equal rights, with both qualities.

Q. *Richard, I have a deep longing for this wild, healthy masculinity. Can you describe it a bit more?*

A. We spent a very beautiful weekend right here in Zurich
with forty men. And when the weekend was over, we
couldn't fully describe male energy. This much for now:
The journey of the wild man, as I call it, calls for the primacy of action, even if we behave falsely. The mistakes we
make are the best teachers in the world. In Greek mythology the young heroes always set forth to do great deeds,
to have adventures. This journey does not take place in
the head. And woman, the fairy tale princess, the "anima"
is not discovered till the end of the journey. In American
movies you always see the women seduced right away in
the first scene; there is no journey, no action, no risks. And
for this reason there's also no genuine encounter with the
opposite. We called our center in New Mexico the Center for Action and Contemplation. Many Christians in the

United States keep asking me, shouldn't it be "Contemplation and Action"? And I always say no. I deliberately put
action at the beginning, because we have nothing we can
become contemplative about until we've done something.

If our father told us we weren't allowed to make any
mistakes, if we were turned into good boys too soon, then
we would repress the longing for this journey because it
frightens us too much. After all, we might make a mistake,
we might not be perfect, we might not be good boys.

The beginning of the masculine journey is taking the risk
upon yourself and going down your path in some quite real
and practical way. The primacy of practice means coming
up with the energy to enter into a concrete commitment in a
concrete situation that demands daring, or where suffering
and repression are involved. And then you can come back
and "taste" it. The most familiar thing said about Mary is
that she "kept all these things in her heart." We teach contemplative prayer, because it's the only way to make a place
big enough to collect all your experiences, so that you don't
need to judge them. You can simply let everything *be:* good
and evil, dark and light, male and female. All that is your
teacher. If we pass judgment too soon and refuse to take
risks, then we will never become spiritually adult.

2   Community Life as a Challenge

BACK HOME IN AMERICA they say anyone is an expert who comes from more than three hundred miles away. That's the only reason I'm the expert today. In any event I'd like to speak from the standpoint of the experiences that I've had thus far.

Perhaps some of you know that I was the founder and (for fourteen years) the pastor of a community in Ohio. Four years ago I had a wonderful contemplative year. After that I headed off to New Mexico, where I've founded a new center. Our center in Albuquerque is not so much a community as a training center for people who work with the poor and oppressed. We try to bring together concerns with spirituality and concerns with social justice.

Around the beginning of the 1970s I was very busy with the "community of communities" (a network of American base communities). Of the fifteen or so communities that joined forces then, only two are still in existence as communities: "New Jerusalem" in Cincinnati and "Sojourners" in Washington, D.C. Whenever I talk with Jim Wallis about this, we both find it very painful, and we rack our brains

---

An afternoon colloquium in Basel, March 8, 1990 (the audience consisted mostly of members of Christian communities and brotherhoods).

over it, wondering why so many communities started up and then folded.

The most plausible answer I've found so far runs like this: They tortured themselves to death. But I also think they had a hard time integrating spirituality and commitment to social justice issues. Some of them developed too much into "therapeutic communities" and imploded. After two or three years many members asked themselves: "What am I still doing here, actually?" Many of the once politically oriented communities collected a crowd of idealists, and then wore each other out with their idealism. Often they were more in love with their own ideals than with reality. If people haven't gone on a serious spiritual journey it's easy to predict that they'll be more in love with the idea of community than with the real thing.

I keep saying to new groups that it's very important from the beginning to be extremely honest about the real expectations and presuppositions that you bring with you. Of course it takes a long time before we discover what these are, especially because so many of these communities have been founded by young people. In a culture like ours, where people grow up very slowly, the communities undeniably turned into places where you worked out your identity problems.

The same thing, of course, is true today about the preparation for religious life. The novice masters of religious orders, more than many other professions, have to grapple with an immense fluctuation in numbers. It's very hard to hold onto twenty-year-olds who are just then becoming adults. It's also difficult because many young people simply use these communities to grow up in. But if we take the capitalistic nature of our culture into consideration, this can scarcely surprise us. Nowadays most things are looked on simply as means of expanding or enriching your own ego. Thus community too can easily become one consumer item alongside others; and once I've consumed it, naturally I can leave it behind. Unfortunately the same rule holds at times even for marriage.

Society is no longer automatically the bearer of the fundamental assumptions that earlier created long-term, stable community. For example, we religious have taken solemn vows, but people find it increasingly hard to understand that. This definitely holds true for celibacy, less for poverty. More and more people acknowledge the need to lead a simple life. In the Reagan era or yuppie era greed became acceptable in polite society. There is new appreciation for serving others instead of merely pursuing your own career. Thank God, we are being greatly influenced by our people who have visited Central America, especially El Salvador and Nicaragua. Many of the missionaries come back and tell us what's going on in the base communities there. We're convinced that the North American Church will be converted by the Latin American Church.

After I had been engaged for fourteen years in a community of committed members, I deliberately wanted to do something different in New Mexico. Our main intention was not to found a community, but to gather people who had a vision of service to the world, to train them and make them qualified for this work. We were confident that in so doing another kind of community would come into existence as a by-product. Now after three and a half years we're very happy with the results. We notice that we're looking in the same direction and that in the process we're joining hands, because it's necessary — and almost accidental. We don't rack our brains so much about *how* to join hands. Many of our communities have, as I said, worried themselves to death, because every morning we kept sticking the thermometer in our mouths to take the community's temperature.

I really believe that the Gospel calls the whole world to a kind of community, to the possibility of a life that can be shared. But community is an art form, and there are obviously many possible ways of getting together. I know many religious in America who live in monasteries but who don't have the capacity for community life: They're too imprisoned in themselves. And at the same time I know many nuns who live alone in apartments and are totally community-oriented, who are bound up and interconnected with the life of many people. The secret lies in the way you let other people get to you, and the way you go out of yourself. This is, of course, at once the mystery of spirituality and the mystery of vulnerability and powerlessness. When a person is on a serious inner journey to his or her own powerlessness, and meanwhile is in immediate contact with the powerless men and women of the world, then community will result.

If one of the two is lacking, people won't be community-oriented. Without an interior life and what we call "love of justice" most communities just serve themselves. We have to look out for this particularly in our country, because we're by nature rather narcissistic. We've had enough leisure to contemplate our belly buttons. Because so many families break up, many people naturally enter communities to experience there the family they never had. That's understandable, but I'm convinced that people have to be called to a vision outside themselves — for the sake of their own healing. Up to a certain point, even if not totally, we get healed and liberated despite ourselves — as a by-product, as I said. We can't spend our whole life working primarily to heal ourselves, because that's grace, it's a gift. This doesn't mean that we shouldn't take the time to work at our problems, but I believe the therapeutic society has its limits.

QUESTIONS and ANSWERS

Q. *What does the way of life in your center look like? How does it differ from traditional communities?*

A. The metaphor that stands behind our whole center is the metaphor of a school for prophets. True, it's not written over our front door, but that's what some people call us. It's my wish (and I hope this is good Franciscan theology) to remain in the Church, but at the same time to be as far out on the inner edge of the Church as possible. Fortunately many bishops and religious superiors have supported me. Thus we were given the possibility of making a place where people could be trained for creative criticism — but on the foundation of faith. It's interesting that we've encouraged all the charisms in the Church — except the charism for prophecy.

The people come to us for so-called practicums, which last between two weeks and two months. And all year long we run many retreats, seminars, workshops, etc. The people write to us and we try to develop an individual program based on their needs.

The essential thing about such programs is always the immediate contact with the poor and oppressed, for example, in prisons, with the homeless, with refugees or battered women, and various other ways. In the afternoon and evening group work and instruction are held in the center, followed by discussion. Every participant has a mentor and a personal spiritual guide who helps him or her to digest what's going on. The crucial points of instruction lie in the realm of liberation theology, i.e., reading the Bible with the eyes of the Third World or women instead of with the eyes of clerics.

We stress contemplative prayer a great deal, because we have the feeling that we're already overstuffed with words and we've argued too long about rituals. Of course the Catholic Church demands that the eucharistic celebration be led by a priest. That's why we Catholics are afraid of forms of prayer that make priests as spiritual leaders superfluous — this happens, for instance, in Latin America. The main reason, though, is that we need forms of prayer that free us from fixating on our own egos and from identifying with our own thoughts and feelings. We have to learn to become spiritually empty. And I see nothing apart from contemplative prayer with the power to accomplish that. This is something that we're absolutely clear about, more than anything else; and it has already yielded very good spiritual fruit.

Every day in the center begins with a twenty-minute contemplative "session": We sit and keep silence. We also teach social analysis at the center. Americans are inclined to be pretty naive: We think somebody is either an American or a communist. Fortunately that's changed somewhat now, because we can no longer simply label the Russians as enemies. So we try to give people a more accurate analysis of society, to help them interpret events in the world. Our conclusion isn't left or right, but the option for the poor. If you begin to analyze things intellectually, you always find truth on both sides. But we think the Gospel has given us a clear directive to stand on the side of those who are the victims. We call this the "bias toward the bottom."

I give a long course called "The Spirituality of Subtraction," in which I've tried to bring psychology, theology, and politics under one roof, and to acknowledge how we have to let go in all realms of life. Particularly as Westerners, we don't have practice in letting go. Even the churches, I think, have taught a spirituality of addition and not subtraction, a one-sided endeavor to get proofs of grace and to achieve salvation. I always thought the Protestants had reformed us Catholics in this area, but I've come to believe they're just as bad. We're all capitalists, and we've expounded the Gospel from the perspective of our capitalistic assumptions, which always leave the ego in the center and make everything into a consumer product. It's amazing how quickly a spirituality of subtraction becomes evident to people. I believe we're in the process of recognizing our shadow side, our addiction to *addition*.

Q. *You're always talking about letting go. How is that done? How does one become powerless?*

A. First, you don't make up your mind to do it. If you deliberately set your sights on it, that will only strengthen your own ego. We can't convert ourselves; we get converted. We have to settle in the world in such a way that circumstances, Reality, can get at us. We're all white Anglo-Saxon Catholics with the same education and biases. That way no one gets converted, everybody legitimizes everybody else in whatever stage of "non-conversion" each one is in.

Ekklesia really means "those who have been called out." But we didn't get called out, we got called in. On Good Friday this year we will set up stations of the cross through the whole city. We'll begin in front of the court house ("Jesus is condemned to death"), and then go to the prison ("Jesus falls for the first time"). This is the first year we're doing this. The idea of doing the stations of the cross as a political act was picked up by the people in all the churches with great enthusiasm — except for some clerics who told us, "You're pulling the people out of the Church." As if the Church had to take place in the church building. But that assumption is centuries old and very hard to overcome. This would be an example of where the Church has to begin letting go.

But the most important thing for us is just to teach contemplative prayer. In the first classes I have to provide the participants with lots of exercises to do, to bring home to them that they shouldn't identify with their thoughts and feelings. Many of our Christian forms of prayer involve thinking about God or having feelings about God. I believe both these forms are extremely limited. This is understandable because we localize the Gospel in the left side of the brain, which finds it easier to think. Another important thing that we have to let go of is left brain dominance. The left side of the brain always wants to understand and explain everything. It's afraid of entering the "cloud of unknowing."

That's the weakness of theology as long as it's separated from spirituality. For this reason we teach more spirituality than theology; historically it was the other way around. So we probably also have to let go of our need for a clear and comforting theology, because we're being led into mystery. In the final analysis that's why we have to let go of our need to keep everything under control. Most of us are very shocked to discover how great our need to control is.

The three great things that in my opinion we have to let go of are the following. First there is the compulsion to be successful. Second is the compulsion to be right — even, and especially, to be theologically right. That's an ego trip, and because of this need churches have split in half, with both parties the prisoners of their own egos. Finally there is the compulsion to be powerful, to have everything under control. I'm convinced that these are the three demons Jesus faced in the wilderness. And so long as we haven't looked these three demons in the face, we should presume that they're still in charge. The demons have to be called by name, clearly, concretely, practically, spelling out just how imperious and self-righteous we are. This is the first lesson in the spirituality of subtraction.

That lesson also has many social and political implications and leads us to letting go of our political mythologies: for example, that we're the best country in the world, as many Americans believe. Pretty soon we've got to overcome nationalism — there isn't a lot of time left. We also have to give up the compulsion to possess so many things and to have our own private stock of everything. The fact that not every one of us needs our own auto or washing machine would naturally make a good argument for physical community.

Q. *What form of contemplative prayer do you prefer?*

A. The most important form for us is a kind of *prayer of centering*. This form was taught very forcefully in America by the Trappists, and I learned it from them. Seen from the outside it almost looks like a Zen prayer form, because first we're not trying to strengthen the ego. In other words it's not followed by any common prayer. That doesn't mean that common prayer isn't in order; we practice it in other places. But we've discovered that on every morning we knew there would be community prayer we wound up reflecting on how to formulate some beautiful prayer. Also we generally don't attach any importance to social activities like drinking coffee or tea afterward; there are other opportunities for that. So these prayer meetings don't offer you any sort of reward, either social or ego-related. There's also no beautiful music playing to produce good feelings. So the world of feeling is not rewarded. You just sit there in silence.

I live in Albuquerque a block away from the house where the Quakers meet. Only thirty people belong to this community, but I'd argue that these thirty people have more influence than most of the other churches put together. Their only form of prayer is to get together and sit there silently, waiting for God's gift. They don't theologize, they don't talk, and they don't even perform any sort of ritual. They simply let go of their ego so God can take over. If you are filled with yourself, there is no room for another, certainly not God. I think these groups have a lot to teach us, especially in the Western churches.

Q. *For me letting go has a lot to do with trust, and I'm often blocked by fear. How can you master this fear?*

A. First, I wouldn't advise you to try to master it. That doesn't mean there might not be another place for doing that. But you can't fix the soul. You can only acknowledge your own rage and your fear of trusting and refuse to identify with it. Because we've lost the art of detachment, we're now an addictive society. When I was a Franciscan novice, we learned a great deal about this distancing, but in the last twenty years we've not been talking about it in my order any more. That's the reason we're tied down to things. Unless we learn to let go of our feelings, then we don't have feelings, the feelings have us. We have to ask: Who is the "I" that has these feelings? The spiritual journey leads us back to this "I." But most men and women in the West have never encountered it. They've become identified with their stream of consciousness, with their feelings. Don't misunderstand me: I'm not saying that you should suppress and deny your feelings. I'm challenging you to name them, identify them, and observe them. But don't fight them and don't identify with them. Teaching this art means teaching contemplative prayer in its first stages.

Now you might ask: What does this have to do with God anyway? All we can do is to get ourselves out of the way — and we can't even do that on our own. That too is something that happens to us, but we have to learn not to take ourselves so seriously. Once we're empty, there is room for God.

Bring your emotions and your mistrust to the Lord as your personal powerlessness. Say: "God, I can't not be enraged, I can't trust!" That's your emptiness. In other words you name your rage and admit it, but you don't identify with it or let it identify with you. This is a great freedom that, in my view, links up good psychology with good spirituality.

Q. *After these training courses how are people supposed to do concrete political work? And what does this concrete work with people on the margin of society look like?*

A. I've already mentioned that all our trainees have a mentor and a spiritual advisor. We have no predetermined goal for the people. The mentors and the spiritual advisors together with the people in question work out what it is they can concretely do when they return home. The only "prejudice" that we have and permit — because we're not neutral, and we've indulged in the illusion of being neutral all too long — leads us to want to help the people find a place alongside the powerless. They will be their teachers. This viewpoint will also keep changing them. I don't know why it took so long for us to see that. Maybe I'm blind too, but for me this is the only way the Gospel makes sense. It's not primarily a political position, but it's also a political position, as you can see from the example of Central America. I've been told that there have been more martyrs there in the last twenty years than in first two centuries of the Roman Church — simply because they were on the side of the poor (which is probably where the early Church was too!).

Q. *That still isn't concrete enough for me. If people in South America change their standpoint and go over to the side of the poor, then that has to express itself in wholly concrete political actions, going along with people to demonstrations, taking part in social struggles, and so on.*

A. Do you mean civil disobedience, going to jail, nonviolent resistance, all those things? In the courses and dialogues we constantly deal with these subjects. At this moment two of our people are "companioning" the people in El Salvador, because the government there has considerable inhibitions about killing *Americans,* since we're giving them a million dollars a day. Some of us at the center have already been in jail. We're strongly convinced that forms of civil disobedience and non-violent resistance are necessary. But we don't tell the people when and where and how they should do it. We just teach them a process for listening.

Two of the three atomic laboratories in America are in New Mexico: Los Alamos, where the atomic bomb was invented, and Kirkland, right in the city of Albuquerque. Every Friday morning we stand at the gates where eighteen thousand workers pour in to work, and we hold up posters presenting questions of faith. We try not to be self-righteous or accusatory; we simply raise issues. Fortunately this has led to a highly respected dialogue with the people who work there; as far as I know, it's the only such dialogue in the country. We prefer this approach, namely first posing questions and then inviting people to dialogue, although the pointed prophetic finger has its justification and its place.

Q. *What has been your experience with the power of the secular and church authorities in your country? How do they judge your work, or do they oppose it? Because for America it's a very new form of community and religious life.*

A. For some reason I've had a great deal of luck, and I've been very blessed. Though I've often spoken out critically, I'm one of the most accepted retreat masters for bishops and priests in our country. That surprises me too. Why do they invite me? I think and hope that they know I'm a son of the Church, that I don't stand outside it. I think they trust me, that my theology is solid — I hope it is too — and that I don't voice criticism irresponsibly for its own sake. Positive and negative criticism have a different energy and personality. I never planned to become like this. But I'm thankful when people say that's how it is. I think St. Francis and Franciscan spirituality have taught me a great deal about how you reform from within.

When I was still a very young priest, Archbishop Bernardin of Cincinnati, who's now cardinal of Chicago, took me under his wing. "Do what you have to do," he told me, "but don't make a movie about it. Don't force me to intervene." He has a wonderful ability to distinguish between dogmatic truth and pastoral practice. Most people apparently can't make this distinction. They think what they have to say is really the objective reality. He had enough discernment of spiritual realities to keep the two apart. He helped me off to a good start.

My Franciscan superior said to me: "Richard, keep on making tapes; just don't write any books." In America I became known mostly through cassettes, not through books. Only in Europe do they make books out of my recordings. The superior thought that the Church's magisterium would need at least twenty years to catch up with my cassettes — they can't call cassettes heresy. So if I get into trouble, it will definitely be on account of my German books.

Q. *Is the make-up of your co-workers bound to any one denomination?*

A. We call ourselves Catholic ecumenists. About 70 percent of the people who come to us are in fact Catholic. But that's connected with the fact that in our region Catholics have more of a social conscience on the issues. The Latin American Church is in the process of radicalizing the Catholic Church in the U.S.A. But the other 30 percent come from all other confessions. The Mennonites and Quakers are very happy because they simply can't believe that we're Catholic. They say, "You talk like we do!"

But even in many theological training centers in the country it turns out that historical denominational differences are becoming less and less significant. We even call that "the European question." And we wonder, why do we have to saddle ourselves with the historical issues?

Those people who have pressed forward to the question of *justice* have discovered that you can work together all day long without knowing what denomination the other person belongs to. Once you've crossed the line to the perspective of justice, you find yourself looking at your denomination and your traditions quite differently. There's a surprising agreement on goals and less arguing about formulations of belief.

Q. *[A nun]: It seems to me that life in some older orders and communities has become rigid these days. I'd like to ask what we can and must learn from the new communities?*

A. There are already grounds for hope in the fact that many men and women who live in older communities are as free as you are and pose that kind of question. I find the same humility and openness to such issues among many American sisters. In our country the nuns are even playing the leading role. In my childhood we always imagined the sisters as harmless, pious creatures. And now nobody is stronger than the sisters, because they're the only ones who have lived real community and who have reciprocally educated one another in the process. Their missionaries came back and opened their eyes for the poor. Of course, within the Church they were in the position of the oppressed, vis-à-vis the clergy. And so they had, and they have now, an advantage over the priests who are continually forced to maintain the system.

The sisters sometimes develop very creative forms of community, and they're even ready, if need be, to give up their canonical status. When they do, a surprisingly large number of them notice that their communities originally had no canonical status at all, in other words they weren't recognized by the Church — and that often their foundresses hadn't even intended to get that status. They're content to be lay women who live in community. These communities increasingly include married couples and single people who haven't taken a vow of celibacy. This may be compared to what originally was the "Third Order."

I believe you've got to trust your own experience and your own heart, and take risks. I think there will always be a form of celibate life in the Church. It has historically borne too much fruit for it not to continue; but it's obviously not the only possible mode of community life. In our center I'm the only one with a vow of celibacy. All the others are married or single people without vows. It's a lay movement. I repeat: We place no special emphasis on community in the formal sense or as an end in itself. It's a by-product of people heading in the same direction.

Q. *What is the difference between sound therapy and incarnation?*

A. You've probably already grasped the right answer intuitively, or else you wouldn't have phrased the question that way. The problems of the spirit can't be resolved with the brain. We have to move in the direction of a more body-related therapy and in the process give more weight to the right half of the brain. We also have to find forms of therapy more oriented to action. We deliberately named our center the center for "action and contemplation," putting

action first. We learn and are healed by committing ourselves. Yet this is an act of faith for which we can show
no proof. Self-oriented persons would prefer not to believe
this. They always want to go rummaging about in their own
souls. It's hard to get people across this borderline.

I recall the early days of New Jerusalem: There were
many people who were strongly influenced by the charismatic movement. They were possessed by the idea of
getting healed, and they constantly refused to be there for
others, because they first had to become whole themselves.
Once they were whole, they'd help others. I'm not ex-
aggerating: To this day these people are still not healed
and they're still waiting. Their narcissism prevents them
from ever being healed. In the last fifteen years we've often replaced spirituality with therapy. We have to see the
limits of the therapeutic society without denying its positive gift. Good psychology has nothing we need to be
afraid of.

Q. *You said the thing was to oppose rituals. What is the role
of the priest in prayer? Is it important for him to be there?*

A. More precisely, what I said was that we have to guard
against *too many* rituals. I hope we're living in a world
where there's a both-and. This means that if we want to
correct an imbalance, we don't immediately have to fall
into the other extreme. Most people at our center say that
the monthly eucharistic celebration is now, as it has been,
our most important get-together. Our daily gathering in the
center is for contemplative prayer. We hold a Eucharist only
once a month. I think these services are very beautiful,
because many different gifts and services come into play
there. We don't deny the role of the priest in them, but nei-

ther do we glorify it. Liturgy in Greek means "the work of the people."

We don't need pyramids, we need circles. Pyramids don't create community. The same is true for the priest. He too needs a place where he can be a brother like all the others. After fourteen years as a retreat master for priests I know that there are too many wrecked priests who are the victims of the pyramid. The priesthood needs liberation for the sake of its own recovery; they have to be invited back into the Christian community.

Q. *In 1987 I visited New Jerusalem after you had left. The people there struck me as rather disoriented. How is this community now? You've spoken very pessimistically about such communities. What future do you see for them?*

A. As a founder, one has a wonderful but also terrible gift: You're able to hold a community together almost despite yourself. But I probably should have gone sooner. Because by staying for fourteen years I put off the necessity of forming a lay leadership that came from the group itself. After I left they went through three painful years. The people had to decide: What do we really want? And not just: What does Richard want? They chose three very good lay pastors. In the past they carried out some very prophetic actions: the community's first house, where I lived after we moved into that part of the city, was placed at the disposal of refugees from Central America. So I believe they're finding their way and their direction again. But dark times are among the best teachers.

3   Getting Rid of the Church

W HAT I'M GOING TO SAY ON THIS SUBJECT will be said in
the context of who and what I am: I'm a man of the
Church; I'm a Franciscan; I'm a priest and I'll die as one,
unless they throw me out first. So my words will come, as
it were, "from inside the family" and not from outside.

I would like to begin speaking about the Church with
the largest image possible: I'd like to begin with creation,
because it's God's primary revelation, as Paul says in the
Letter to the Romans: "Ever since the creation of the world
his invisible nature, namely, his eternal power and deity,
has been clearly perceived in the things that have been
made" (Rom. 1:20). Even though we can't see God, we
can discover God in what God has created. That's what
we mean by a "theology of creation": We start not with the
problems that came up later but with what God created. In
the last verse of the first chapter in the Bible it says: "And
God saw everything that God had made, and behold it was
very good" (Gen. 1:31). That's the only time in the whole
Bible that anything is called "very good." But we've been
so busy with the later problem of redemption that we've
forgotten what God said in the very beginning. We are so
trapped in our own tiny moment that we forget the big
picture. And I assume God understands this.

A talk given in the Church of St. Matthew, Basel, March 8, 1990.

In America there was recently a TV program called "Life on Earth," where the whole history of creation was telescoped into a year. The earth began in January. Around April the reptiles made their appearance. In September came the creation of the mammals. I don't remember all the intermediary steps, but I know that we came very late. *Homo sapiens*, the "wise man," as we like to style ourselves, emerged in the last three minutes of December 31. That means that the whole Judeo-Christian tradition was played out in the last milliseconds of December 31.

I can't believe that God was speaking for the first time in those final milliseconds. St. Bonaventure called the creation "God's fingerprint." We've forgotten to read these fingerprints, because we're so busy with our theological theories.

Jesus invites us as the Church to be a new community of human beings; he calls us a little flock. I don't believe he ever wanted us to be the whole. He said we should be the yeast, the leaven, not the whole loaf. He said we should be the salt, but we want to be the whole meal. He said we could be the light that illumines the mountain top, but we want to be the whole mountain. The images that Jesus uses are very modest and yet very strong. It's hard for us, especially in the context of European experience, to resist the temptation to act as if we were "Christianity" all by ourselves. The continent of Europe had the goal of being "Christianity," and hence it's very difficult to be merely leaven and salt and light. We hardly know how to do that. We want to lead; we want the way of power. But the only rules Jesus gave us were the rules of powerlessness. Out of his announcement of a new reality that Jesus called the Reign of God we have made the Church.

When Jesus described this new reality, which he called

the Reign of God, he obviously was *not* talking about the
Church. But the Church — just like the people of Israel —
has continually been tempted to idolize itself. Yet if it
adores itself, it can't adore the One who alone deserves
to be adored. The proclamation of the Reign of God means
that only *one* thing is absolute — everything else is relative. Everything else is a means to the end. That includes
the Church, the Bible, the sacraments, and also all the exercises of spiritual life. None of all that is an end in itself.
As the Zen masters say, they are fingers that point to the
moon. But we spend most of our time arguing over who
has the best fingers and who has the true fingers, instead
of pointing to the moon. This is quite clearly a transgression
of the First Commandment, namely, the worship of idols.

The first image of an idol was made by the first priest,
Aaron. As soon as Moses came down from the mountain,
glowing from the experience of the mystery, his brother
Aaron quickly produced religion by making the golden calf.
That way you have God at your disposal, you have God
in hand, we're in control. The temptation of religion always consists in turning the tables so that we ourselves take
charge of the situation. Thus the first mistake consists in
confusing the Reign of God with the Church. We Catholics
have been especially bad on this score.

The second and more frequent mistake consists in confusing the Reign of God with heaven, as if we went into
God's Reign, or Kingdom, when we die. But Jesus' prayer
says quite clearly: The Kingdom of God is here, "Thy Kingdom come." It's not here in the sense that we could grab
hold of it. "If anyone says to you, 'Lo, here is the Christ,' or
'There he is!' do not believe it" (Matt. 24:23). It will never
be so bound up with any institution or reality that we can
once again be in control. The Reign of God is in every

place where God's truth breaks through into our world. And sometimes there's no signboard hung out in front with "Christian" on it, as Jesus said: "Not everyone who says to me, 'Lord, Lord,' shall enter the kingdom of heaven, but he who does the will of my Father who is in heaven" (Matt. 7:21).

Four hundred years later St. Augustine said: "Many belong to the Church who do not belong to God. And many belong to God who do not belong to the Church." That's no new theology; it describes what happens when we want to put God in our pockets or when we try to table the issue till eternity. The challenge is to do what Jesus did, namely, to accept what's Real, to welcome it into this transitory world. And whenever you do that, you pay a price, because then you normally have to let go of your "little kingdoms" — the kingdoms of power, the kingdoms of prestige, and the kingdoms of possessions.

The harshest words of Jesus are aimed at hypocrites, and the second harshest at the people who are primarily concerned with possessions. He says that power, prestige, and possessions are the three things that prevent us from recognizing and receiving the Reign of God. When he says that to good, upright people, their reaction is indignation and scandal. They call him an unbeliever, an enemy of the law, and finally a devil — because they *own* too many things that they have to defend. The only ones who can accept the proclamation of the Reign are those who have nothing to protect, neither their own self-image nor their reputation, their possessions, their theology, their principles, nor their certitudes. And these are called "the poor," *anawim* in Hebrew. In the Magnificat Mary sums up the spirituality of the *anawim*.

If in this world we are already living in the reality of

the Reign of God, then the world becomes relative and we become "pilgrims and strangers." Life can't be based on the passing, it can't be based on transitory images. Instead, you know you have to base it on the truth, on the truth of who you are, on the truth of this creation, which God says is "very good."

Our problem consists in the fact that we're so conscious of *not* being good. And you need a great deal of trust to believe God's pronouncement that everything God created is very good. We seem to believe that only perfect things are lovable — that's our problem. Yet the Gospels say very clearly that God loves imperfect things. But it's only the imperfect and the broken who can believe that. Thus it happens that God throws a party — and the "good" people don't come. That's why God says that the cripples, the lame, and the blind are to be invited — and they would be ready.

This pattern has never changed. Those who don't have anything to prove or protect can believe that they are loved, as they are. But we who have spent our lives ascending the spiritual ladder or some other ladder can't hear the truth. For the truth isn't up at the top, but down at the bottom. And by trying to climb the ladder we miss Christ, who comes *down* through the Incarnation. I'm convinced that many of the guilt feelings the middle class is haunted by, much of its widespread poor self-image, as we call it, and much of its self-hatred and self-centeredness are due to the fact that we live in, and have settled down in, a world that Jesus says we should never be at home in. If you base your life on illusion, you will naturally hate yourself. The proclamation of the Reign of Heaven is the most radical political and theological statement that could ever be made. It has nothing to do with being perfect. It has to do with basing our life on the Real. And for *all* of us that means we have to change our lives. Not only to think differently or to attend a particular kind of church service or to live with a new kind of theology of redemption. We don't think our way into a new life; we live our way into a new kind of thinking. The Gospel is before all else a call to *live* differently, so that life can be shared with others.

I believe that the religion of the middle class was always tempted to use Scripture primarily to dispense consolation. But the Word of God, like a mirror, must first *confront* us with ourselves. Second, it has to *challenge* us to live in a new way, to lead a life of authentic brotherliness and sister-liness — economically, politically, socially, and spiritually. Only after the Word of God has confronted and challenged us do we have the right to take *consolation* from the Word of God as well. But we've drawn consolation from the Bible before we changed our lives! The Christian nations are among the greediest and the most intent on security of any in the world, while they maintain that Jesus is their Lord and their security.

I've had the opportunity to preach in many parts of the world. A non-Christian once told me: "Why should we be-lieve in your Christ? You Christians have waged the most wars, you use up the most resources in the world, and you've raped the planet. And then you say you love your poor Jesus. You hate Jesus and only say you love him to fool yourselves." I have no answer to this, because I know it applies to me. Over large parts of this planet Christianity and the Church have increasingly less credibility. If we're honest, we have to admit that we've turned them into the-ories of redemption and psychic trips. For us the Gospel has never really landed on earth; it's never touched the socio-political and economic order; the Kingdom of God never came. False religion comes on the scene when we piously say, "Thy Kingdom come," but don't immediately add, "My kingdom go." And we Christians have believed that we could both say, "Jesus is Lord!" and go on being the lords of our own lives. That's "the lord of the flies."

We want to say, "Jesus is Lord!" and still believe, as Americans do, that we are the most significant nation in the world. That sort of Gospel isn't credible, and neither is that sort of Church.

I'm convinced that we were busy worshipping the messenger so we could ignore the message. The greatest part of the Sermon on the Mount has never been taken seriously — neither by Catholic nor by Protestants. All of us have to be reformed. But I believe that we're little people; God is too big for us. As far as our readiness to hear the Gospel goes, we have perhaps grown a year per century. That means we're about at the point of turning twenty. We're just about to become adults and to honestly let the Gospel speak to us — to listen to what Jesus says, in no uncertain terms, about poverty and about leading a simple life in this world, a life that trusts in God and not in our own power and weapons. And yet we're now spending 60 percent of our resources to "protect" ourselves, although God never promised us security in this world. God promised us only truth and freedom in our hearts. But we didn't want the Reign of God, we didn't want the "Pax Christi." We wanted the "Pax Romana," we wanted triumphal Christianity.

What does all this mean for us? It means that we're on the way. It does no good to hate ourselves. We stand on the shoulders of our forebears and bear the burden of their sins and the fame of their holiness. They are an image of what we are, and we are an image of what they were. When you head out on the inner journey of faith, then you will discover that you are exactly the same: You will find many things in yourself that you're afraid of and that you don't like — if you're really honest. But if you remain on the way, you will also find a part of yourself that you know is very good, you will discover *who we are in God*. You don't earn that, it's what you are. This is a net that you can't fall out of.

To preach the Reign of God, dear brothers and sisters, we have to break with our *dependency on* a perfectible self. People who have suffered, people who are twisted out of shape, people who are oppressed have a lead on us. Those of us who are good, sound, and strong have a hard time getting out of the starting blocks.

If you suffer and are confronted by limits, you know that reality isn't perfect. You know that from below, from your gut and not just from your head. Your trust is not in "progress" but in mercy.

A few years ago I heard the following story in America: William Casey, the head of the CIA, had just died. He was a good Irish Catholic, and his good Irish wife was on TV that evening. Around that time the newspapers had already begun to discover a lot of corruption in the CIA. (We think, for example, we have the right to rub out leading figures in the world if it serves our national security interests.) Now Mrs. Casey said that anyone who raised questions about her dear husband was committing blasphemy. As a good Irish Catholic, she really must have known the definition of blasphemy. Blasphemy doesn't mean defaming the CIA, but defaming God. But when a country makes itself God — and on that point you're as bad as we are — then we can't hear the Gospel. Then we use Christ to prop up our own nation-state. Then we use the Church to bless the nation-state and its illusions.

You now see how dangerous it is to believe in the Gospel — and why Jesus said,"The world will hate you" (John 15:19). I have to ask — we all have to ask — "Does the world hate us?" There's nothing to hate, because most of the time we play the same game as all the others. We haven't built our lives on a new reality, we've built it on the same old reality as all the others: power, prestige, and possessions.

We can't make up our minds to convert — we *get* converted. We get converted despite ourselves. We can only ask to be able to live with open hands, to become practiced and prepared in the art of letting go, so that the Gospel can teach us how to be poor in this world — with nothing that we have to prove or protect. Jesus says: "It will be good news for the poor," but not for those who have a lot to defend (see Luke 4:18).

In large parts of the universal Church something wonderful is happening: Many people are coming to hear the proclamation of the Reign of God and to commit themselves to issues of justice. And in the process we notice that the historical questions raised by the different denominations are not the important ones. The questions of the Reformation were mostly questions of educated white male clerics — and they were questions of power and justification. Who has the power and who's right? That's what adolescents argue about. But we're twenty years old now, and we're ready to listen to the more substantial questions about the Gospel, questions about community, about non-violence, questions about loving one's enemies, about leading a poor and simple life in this world — points that Jesus expressed his opinion on quite unequivocally. His statements about the sacraments and the priesthood are much less clear. We've never burned people as heretics for not caring about the least of their brothers and sisters, although it does say in Matthew 25 that this is the only thing we'll be judged on.

For a long time I thought I'd be judged on how many Masses I'd gone to. And until a few years ago I always had an irreproachable Sunday balance sheet. I thought I'd be judged on how perfect I was and how I had kept the Ten Commandments. I was quite disappointed to discover Matthew 25, because God doesn't even mention it there. And yet I had a pretty good record that I could have shown God. God says, "Did you recognize Christ *in the least* of your brothers and sisters?" By the way, this is the only time in Scripture that the same thing is repeated four times in a row, so that we can't miss the point — and still we've managed to do just that. We come back and ask, "But when did we see you hungry and thirsty?" Evidently it seems we don't even have to know that we're doing it for Jesus (fundamentalists beware!). We only have to do the truth. In creation God has revealed what God is. And if we meet this creation in its brokenness and its poverty, we meet "Christ in his most distressing disguise," as Mother Teresa says.

Let me close with some practical encouragement: Many of us first take the outward journey and discover outside of us a reality that's broken or poor or wretched — and in the process we learn compassion for ourselves. Many of us begin from within and are driven outward, but in either case we have to go *the whole way*. If you go the whole way inward, there too you'll discover something that's broken and poor and in need of compassion. In the language of St. Francis this is called "the leper within us." Francis couldn't bear to see lepers. But he says in his Testament that as soon as he embraced the first leper what once had been hateful to him became "sweetness and life."

Many of us first have to learn to embrace the leper within us before we can embrace the leper outside. In the final analysis it's the same act of compassion. And it's not a compassion that we produce, but a compassion that's given to us.

Many of us were brought up in a totalitarian spirituality, not in a spirituality of compassion. "Kill the enemy, attack the enemy!" — and so we've attacked and killed ourselves. But if we learn a new spirituality of non-violent compassion toward our own soul, we'll have the same present to offer the world. As I mentioned yesterday, many groups outside the Church are discovering this better than the Church itself. And that may be the reason the churches have become so weak. We're busy with power, with spiritual power, and many of the "little ones" of this world have discovered powerlessness. I mentioned in particular the program of Alcoholics Anonymous and the Twelve Step program. I believe these groups are in many ways a model for what the mystery of the Church could be. And the decisive first point is the radical experience of one's own powerlessness, which drives you into a circle of men and women who share the same experience. And I believe this is the fundamental mystery of the Church: Two or three gather in his name and perhaps without saying his name at all — because his name is broken, bleeding flesh. And if we surrender ourselves to this experience, we betake ourselves into the flesh of Christ. In other words, Christ redeems us all despite ourselves. No tradition and no Church will triumph before God. We all stand there in need of eternal compassion. In short, it is the two poverties that convert us: the poor man/woman within and the poor man/woman without. They drive toward one another.

QUESTIONS and ANSWERS

Q. *Can you say something further about communities?*

A. By community I mean first of all living in such a way that others can get through to me and influence my life and I can get out of myself and serve their life. Community is about a world where brotherliness and sisterliness are possible. By community I don't mean primarily a special kind of structure, but a network of relationships. On the whole we live in a society that's built not on community and cooperation, but on competition.

Q. *Wouldn't it be nice to get together like the first Christians in a house Church, especially with people who are at home with themselves, who know their good sides and their shadow sides? Do you know any of these house churches in the U.S.A. or in Europe?*

A. In the New Testament we see precisely what you call a house Church — and it was probably about forty people. I've been tremendously influenced by what's happening in Latin America and by the reciprocal relationship between the base communities and the institutional Church. If we have only the institutional Church, everything very quickly becomes formalized, legalistic, and unreal. But if you have only the base communities, then you often have what Americans call a flash in the pan. These communities are normally successful for a short time, but history has shown us that they quickly become narrow and sectarian. I'm convinced that we grow best when we live in a creative tension between the two types of Church and idolize neither of them. The problem is that for four hundred years we've had nothing else but the institutional Church. And we didn't have permission to experiment a lot with base communities. So we have to do it now, even though we'll undoubtedly make some mistakes in the process.

In Brazil alone there are eighty to a hundred thousand base communities. That would never have happened if there had been a whole lot of priests. God had a better idea. And conversely this doesn't mean that the institutional Church is false. But something else has to bring it into equilibrium and keep it honest. I'm sure that most of you come from reformed churches that in the beginning and summation were on fire. But in the end every community recapitulates the whole path of conversion. That's why my advice for most people is to blossom where they were planted and to deal with realities in little groups, but to remain connected somehow or other with the institution. The institution is the point where history is at in 1990. And we have to stay in dialogue with history, because the institution will still be there when our little groups have long since passed away. At bottom this has something to do with respect and love for our ancestors, however strange that may sound. I always have to tell Americans this because they think that we're the beginning and summation of history.

Q. *With the house groups there's often a danger that we'll remain too concentrated on ourselves. I think it's terrific when people in such groups face the whole reality and find the balance between observing their own souls and staying in clear-eyed contact with the world.*

A. When I spoke this afternoon to several community groups, I talked about the danger of becoming a purely therapeutic community that revolves around its own ego.

The act of our faith consists in donating and giving away what we don't yet have — that's why it's faith. That's so hard for us to understand: How can I give away something that I don't even have? Nevertheless I go out and heal others, even though I myself am not yet healed. I heal them through my brokenness, not through my power! Every church community that doesn't include an outwardly directed service for others, a service extending beyond itself, is simply not a Church, it's not Christ. It's psychology or false transcendence. That doesn't mean that psychology is a bad thing; it just isn't the same thing.

Q. *I really had a little panic attack: the institution as the balancing factor. If you're talking about the Alcoholics Anonymous model — and I'm a member — AA is not bound up with any institution. Still, it's connected with the world as a whole, with life — above and beyond its groups. Couldn't that be a model too? The most important factor after all is being in contact with the world as a whole and not just constantly running in circles around yourself.*

A. The original meaning of the word "Catholic" is to be bound up with our past and the future and not to get lost in ourselves. But in this sense most Catholics have never been Catholic. They were very racist and nationalistic. And yet we have to keep on trying. Today perhaps instead of "Catholic" we say "global" or "planetary" or wholistic. That has nothing to do with the "New Age." It's simply creation spirituality that we can read about in the Book of Genesis. In Revelation we are told that Christ is the Alpha and the Omega, the beginning and end of history. Insofar as a small group has the capacity to tie in with God's history, I think it's a healthy one.

Q. *You're here in the city of Karl Barth. If we think back fifty years, what would have become of the Church if it hadn't had theologians reflecting on the kerygma, with the courage to say the word that the world didn't want to listen to? So my question is: In the context of Europe mightn't this old institution of the Protestant Church, reborn from Luther, have an important role to play in our confused times?*

A. Only God knows, I don't. But I suspect that the movement of church history today doesn't have its center in Europe. All the signs speak against it. Nowadays 70 percent of all Christians live in the Third World. We've had our chance on the stage. Now the Bible has to be interpreted through the eyes of women, through the eyes of the poor, and through the eyes of a communitarian picture of the world, as I've found in Africa, through a more body-centered spirituality and through a more contemplative spirituality, as you can find in Asia. This doesn't mean that we were wrong, just that there are many other parts of the mystery of Christ that have to be unveiled. And our part as traditional churches is to be humble enough to let go and to let the other voices have their say.

4   Christians and Political Commitment

O N THE LAST DAY OF THE YEAR, the feast of St. Sylvester, I generally withdraw to pray. So in the final hours of 1989 I asked myself: What should I pray for this year? What do we need in the 1990s? Naturally you're strongly tempted to say that we should pray for more love. But it occurred to me that I've met so many people in the world who are already full of love and so many people who really care for others. I believe that what we lack isn't love but wisdom. It became clear to me that for the 1990s I should pray above all else for wisdom.

We all want to love, but as a rule we don't know how to love rightly. *How* should we love so that life will really come from it? I believe that what we all need, and what East Germany in particular needs, is wisdom. I'm very disappointed that we in the Church have passed on so little wisdom. Often the only thing we've taught people is to think that they're right — or that they're wrong. We've either mandated things or forbidden them. But we haven't allowed people to enter upon the narrow and dangerous path of true wisdom. Because on this path we have to take the risk of making mistakes. On this path we have to take

A talk given in the Church of the Cross, Dresden, March 14, 1990.

the risk of being wrong. That's the great school of wisdom. On the spiritual path the enemy isn't pain; it's *fear* of pain. We haven't become wise, because we're so afraid of pain.

I believe that there are two necessary paths enabling us to move toward wisdom: a radical journey inward and a radical journey outward. For far too long we've held people down in a sort of security zone, at a safe midpoint. We've called them neither to a radical path inward, in other words, to contemplation, nor to a radical journey outward, that is, to commitment on the social issues of our time. Probably because these two great teachers, the inner and the outer way, both cause pain, we prefer to stay in a secure middle position. Failure and falling short are the best teachers; on the spiritual path success has practically nothing to teach. But we notice that many of us incline to the one side or the other, on account of either temperament or education. Wherever I travel to in the Church, I find people who move inward and people who are activists. These two types seldom come together, and thus they both miss half the Gospel, they both lack half the truth.

I feel certain that we in the West have to begin primarily with action. The great temptation of the Western Church has been to imprison the Gospel in our heads. Up there you can be right or wrong, your position can be correct or false, but in any case everything always remains firmly in your grip. Action never allows us the illusion of control, at least not for long.

True action never permits the illusion that we will always understand everything. When we get involved with the pain of this world, we notice very soon that we have only a little fragment of the truth.

It looks as if we are condemned to live in a world that is a mixture of darkness and light, of good and evil. Jesus

spoke of the field in which wheat and weeds grow alongside each other. We say, "Lord, shouldn't we go and rip out
the weeds?" But Jesus says: "No, if you try to do that, you'll
probably rip the wheat out along with the weeds. Let both
grow alongside each other in the field till harvest" (Matt.
13:24–30). You need a lot of patience and humility to live
with this sort of field in yourself. Because in our own souls
both weeds and wheat grow right next to each other.

We'll never win if we launch a frontal assault on evil.
If we do that we may incorporate into ourselves the energy and the weapons of evil. We can end up by turning
into what we hate (see M. Scott Peck, *The People of the Lie*
[New York: Simon & Schuster, 1983]). That's why Jesus told
us we have to love our enemies; otherwise we become just
like them. Hitler once supposedly said that the wonderful
thing about Nazism was that all those who directly attacked
it became fascists themselves in the process. The U.S.A. has
a lofty self-image and thinks it conquered fascism. Nevertheless today America supports extreme right-wing regimes
in Guatemala, El Salvador, and South Africa. You never
see your own sin; you always rationalize your sin away
as virtue. For this reason we need help in recognizing that
we ourselves are a mixture of good and evil.

There is no perfect political system. Jesus never promised us that any political system could realize the Reign
of God on earth. He advised us to take a humble position
in this world, a position of non-participation in the lie. He
called this position "yeast." But we want to be the whole
loaf. He told us we should be the salt in the food, but we
want to be the whole meal. He said we should be the light
on the mountain, but we want to be the whole mountain
(Matt. 5:13ff.).

It's very hard for Christianity to accept a minority position, to do what we have to do with integrity and truth-fulness and leave the future to God. There is no perfect theology, there are no perfect explanations, there is no perfect road leading to psychic health. We are always forced to live in a world that contains both life and death. The Reign of God is already here, but it's not whole yet. Faith means standing in this position and holding on to both sides at the same time. If we take the contemplative path, then we see the shadow side and the inconsistency of our own souls. If we take the path outward, then we head to the place where the victims are. If we try to find out what truth is by arguing, there will always be good arguments on both sides. At some point we must risk the dangerous decision for faith. And that means always standing on the side of the weak, always on the side of the poor, always on the side of the victims. As a rule that will make us unpopular.

If you stand on this side, you'll be misinterpreted by the opposite side. In Central and South America there have been more martyrs in the last twenty years than in the first two hundred years of Christianity. The main reason for their martyrdom was that they stood on the side of the poor. Jesus told us that we would someday be judged by whether we had stood on this side and whether we had recognized and found him there. In Matthew 25 he says that we will be judged by whether we recognized Christ in the least of his brothers and sisters. Jesus' option for the poor is a war of the Lamb. He goes down the "low road" that we're all afraid of.

The Bible is always history from the side of the victims. It begins with the story of the Jews who were dragged into slavery in Egypt. The Bible was written from the perspective of people who were oppressed, who were enslaved, who were poor. It is a partisan presentation of history that takes the side of the losers. But we were overzealous in understanding the story from the side of the *victors!* You yourselves know exactly what that means for you in East Germany. Perhaps it means for all of us that we have to go precisely to the place we're most afraid of, we have to go to the place we're ashamed of, we have to go to the place where we are oppressed, we even have to go where we hate ourselves. Only in that place can we establish the connection between the path inward and the path outward. If we learn to acknowledge and love the poor man and the poor woman in our own soul, we'll understand the truth that is hidden in the poor man and in the poor woman whom we find outside ourselves.

The Bible speaks of four forms of poverty: There is first the poverty of sin, the poverty *before conversion.* In this condition the person is completely empty, the person is missing the truth. For such people the word of God is, "Repent and live!"

The second poverty is the poverty of *oppressed men and women,* whom have no time or no means of living in a way truly worthy of their humanity, for example, the enslaved and abused Israelites in Egypt. And here the word of God issued to Moses is, "Change the situation!" The whole Judeo-Christian tradition begins with God's demand to change history, to oppose the pharaoh. Nevertheless God asks them to wander through the wilderness for forty years and to expose themselves to a process of purification. Here we see the very first connection between the inner journey and the outer journey.

The third poverty the Bible speaks of is the poverty of a *simple and humble life.* It is the challenge of living simply, of placing our hope and our trust in God and in other people instead of in material things. Because we never learned that and never took it seriously, in either the Catholic or the Protestant tradition, we have fallen prey to the totalitarian systems of this century that always *force* us to do what Jesus *asks* us to do freely. It looks as if God always takes the risk of freedom: God too demands, but then God simply waits. God waits as long as necessary until we can love of our own free will. God is not only modest, God is also very patient. The political systems of this world have no patience.

The fourth poverty in the Bible is the deep realization of my own limitedness and weakness. This is the central motif of the Sermon on the Mount: "Blessed are the poor in spirit. Blessed are those who weep" (Matt. 5:3ff.). Many things in life cannot be changed, you can only grieve over them. So long as we are no longer under the *compulsion* of wanting to change them, we have the *freedom* to change them. Then the change comes from much greater depth, not from our anger, but from a place of integrity, not from a place where fear dwells, but from deep trust, not from a place where self-righteousness rules, but from wisdom.

There are at least two different ways to be a prophet. The first is the way that Moses took. His task was to tell enslaved men and women: "You can be free!" The second way is the way of Jesus. To men and women who consider themselves free he says that they are actually enslaved. The second way is much rarer and much harder. I believe that in your historical situation you may need both kinds of prophets. You have to learn to trust a new kind of freedom, but you must also recognize the good that was hidden in your own communist past. You have to unmask the false definition of freedom that the West wants to offer you.

The Gospel says we aren't really free so long as we haven't been freed from ourselves. And no political system can teach us or offer us this freedom. When Mother

Teresa came to America, she called us one of the most un-free peoples in the world. We Americans are paralyzed by all our possibilities. We consider ourselves a tremendous nation because we can choose from a gigantic menu of consumer articles. Even Christians are ready to believe this sort of nonsense. When they do, they avoid traveling through the depths of the wilderness. Our enemy isn't pain, but the fear of pain.

Jesus came to teach us the way of wisdom. He brought us a message that offers to liberate us from both the lies of the world and the lies that are lodged in ourselves. The words of the Gospel create an alternative consciousness, a free and solid ground on which we can really stand, free from every social order and from every mythology. Jesus called this new foundation on which we stand the Reign of God. And he said the Reign of God is something that takes place in this world and yet will never be completed in this world. This means that we're back where we started, with faith. We understand now why Jesus keeps asking: "When the Son of man comes, will he find faith on earth?" (Luke 18:8). It is so rare to be able to endure being where we don't trust the systems of this world or any system, but stand at a place of both light and darkness, at a place where we offer to give our salt, our leaven, our light on the mountain. But we have no security that we're really right. This means that we have to stand at an inconspicuous, mysterious place, which seems more dark than light: "When the Son of man comes, will he find faith on earth?" At the place of faith I'm not sure that I'm sure.

Jesus never promised us security in this world, and yet we're ready to buy any political system that promises us quick and easy security, instead of living in this essential insecurity, in this deep inner poverty, where we really learn something. It's the school of the victims where we learn something, not the school of the winners, not the school of security.

That is why, dear brothers and sisters, I believe that we Christians are becoming an increasingly small group. There are simply fewer and fewer reasons to be Christian on social grounds. For centuries the churches have held the nation-state system together and strengthened it. Christians have often failed to get to a place that wasn't dependent on rulers, dictators, and kings. This is an anxious situation. Without the light of Christ and without faith in the presence of God none of us would want to stand there. "When the Son of man comes, will he find faith on earth?" It's beautiful that in spite of everything we can still give voice to these words in the Church, and that you're ready to lend an ear to such a crazy truth. This shows me that the Church is still a place of hope, that we can preach the folly of the cross.

A Jewish master once said: "God is not nice. God is not an uncle. God is an earthquake." We've created a middle-class version of Christianity that has manufactured a nice God. We want Jesus finally to take away our insecurity. We want to feel as if we were just wheat and not weeds. But God isn't nice, and God isn't an uncle. God is an earthquake. In a way the preaching of the Gospel pulls the rug out from under us. We have to put our life on a new footing. I believe we've always thought that we could reason our way into the Gospel. But we'll never solve the way to a new life in our heads; we have to live our way into a new kind of thinking. First we have to act, we have to dare to cross over this frontier and live differently, so that, starting out from this point we can again ask fresh questions. That's why action and decision come *first*.

I believe the best way to get a real grasp of the truth of the Gospel looks like this: We have to enter into solidarity with at least one person who's different from us. This means crossing over the line to the other side. For example, if you're afraid of a certain race or a certain religion, then the best thing is to head directly there. If you're afraid of certain people, then you have to enter into solidarity with those people. We have to endure being with those people for a while and learn to view reality from their standpoint. That's why Jesus says we have to love our enemies. It's the only way to grasp the whole picture. It's the only way to learn to love the other side of our soul.

But I repeat: Don't try to solve it in your head, simply do it. From the vantage point of this action you'll understand what I mean. The problem isn't solved in the head but in the gut, in the whole body (naturally in the head too, but that doesn't come till later). And that's what I mean when I speak of the risk and the leap of faith. First we have to act — and then we'll understand. Then the whole person will understand. Then I'll know what I know. But I really won't know why I know. I also can't prove to you why I know something; it's the wisdom of faith. It's the wisdom you learn only when you're on the way. This is homework nobody else can do for you, neither the pope nor the Bible; you have to go down this road yourself. That's what the "primacy of action" means. Persist at that deeper place in yourself where the both-and is located. This is the place of the soul, the place of wisdom, toward which we have to move. Don't be afraid! Fear comes from a need to control. And we are not in control anyway.

QUESTIONS and ANSWERS

Q. *I see a contradiction here. We're supposed not to be afraid of being wrong in the eyes of others, but if I follow the principles in our country, I have to try to be right.*

A. Jesus' commandment isn't, "You shall be right," but "You shall love one another." Of course, it's not wrong to be right. The problem begins when we face an inner compulsion always to be the ones who are right. If we're too taken up with this question, then we're continually taken up with our self-image, and such people were precisely the ones who killed Jesus. This is the eternal pattern: the moral high-ground, that is, the compulsion to be right and powerful, killed Jesus! Here we have to make a very delicate distinction: Naturally we should be obedient to God, but we're not supposed to maintain our positive self-image at any price (and sometimes that looks very much like obedience). The genuine saints of every age haven't worried about their own holiness and didn't consider themselves saints.

I have a rule of thumb that says that those who believe they are holy aren't. Jesus says that the prostitutes, the tax-collectors, and the sinners will enter the Reign of God rather than those who sit before him in the synagogue. When Jesus healed sick people and touched them, he always said in the end: "Your faith has made you whole." He never said, "Your correct doctrine, your orthodoxy, your dogmatism have healed you." I too hope, of course, that I'm acting correctly, but I can't continually circle around this question. I have to do what I have to do, and then I can leave the judgment to God. Otherwise I'm under the compulsion to be constantly passing judgment. But those constantly passing judgment are not in a position to perceive their own reality. You immediately organize everything into categories, and that makes it easier for you to have control over the world.

Q. *How can we live without judging? You yourself have criticized American society. You criticize the churches.*

A. Naturally we have to learn to distinguish between darkness and light. But we're never allowed to succumb to the illusion that we ourselves don't have a share in the darkness. The darkness, what we see out there, is always a part of us. I tell people who want to be prophets: You can't play the prophet until you've discovered in yourself what you accuse others of.

You're right about your question, of course. We can't naively skip over the subject of darkness and light. And it's precisely because we were so naive that we so often became victims of dark powers and called them light.

Q. *Isn't dogmatism also an aid for us in groping our way through the darkness in this world, like a sort of staircase?*

A. Our conclusions aren't as important as the *process* we go through. Most of the crimes in this world have been committed by people who thought they were right. Thomas Aquinas says, "All people chose something that seems good to them." We all believe we're right. That's why we have to set off on an inner spiritual path that finally shatters this illusion, the illusion of a world that breaks down into black and white. I'm sure the Nazis imagined *they* were in the right, and the comrades of the SED [Sozialistische Einheitspartei Deustchlands] imagined they were in the right.

That's exactly what I mean when I talk about spiritual journeys. The way inward demands that you build bridges with your own soul. But anyone who builds a bridge always runs the danger of being trampled from both sides, of being misunderstood by both sides. Like the prophets we ourselves stand "in the breach," like them we run the danger of going under. I've never found that a lot of wisdom comes into the world through people who have planted themselves dogmatically somewhere or other.

But I have found that a great deal of wisdom comes into the world through people who humbly stand by with their arms outstretched like a cross, holding on to both sides. I'd like to stress that point here in particular because I believe that you have a unique opportunity to do just that: to hold on to much of the good from the past forty years and nevertheless to be open to the risk of seeing some new good — but not to idolize either of them. That's why it says in the First Commandment that we're not to worship idols. Idols are absolute explanations that give us the feeling of being absolutely right, and then we adore these explanations. Our justice (and this is good Lutheran theology) is always a gift of God and not our own doing. That gift is given to us mostly despite ourselves. But not if we continually ask, "Am I right? Am I right?" Faith doesn't always allow us such quick comfort.

Q. *The spiritual comparison of God with an earthquake moved me deeply. In my own Protestant Church it's so club-like and sober, there's no enthusiasm [an obvious "enthusiast"].*

A. Let me say once more that people who have had strong emotional experiences of God must also dare to step out into the world. The God who has touched them is leading them to do the same. We become like the God we adore. A dogmatic person has a dogmatic God. A compassionate person has experienced the compassion of God. But we also have to help those who are busy at work with the social questions of our time, to get them to take the chance of faith. For this reason it's an earthquake for both. Because each time we have the comfortable ground and foundation we're standing on pulled out from under us. This draws people who are more spiritualized out into the world where they no longer have matters under control. Conversely it leads people who are socially and politically active into an inner world where there is nothing to be done and they likewise no longer have everything under control.

I understand your longing for more emotion, but I'd like to say one more thing: As a rule faith has nothing to do with feeling.

The more we are on the journey of faith, the more faith has to do with trust and self-surrender. The Kingdom of God leaves none of us in our own little kingdom where we decide what happens. God leads us all, like Abraham, out into a new country.

Q. *We Europeans look on truth as a static condition instead of as a process of discovery, in which many things are involved: the body, mental concentration, but also action for the world. Do you agree with me on that?*

A. I myself have German-born parents, and I don't exclude myself from what I'm about to say now: The longer I preach the Gospel on all five continents, the clearer it becomes to me that Europeans, especially the Germans, feel most at ease in their heads. I first got a real awareness of this in Asia and Africa. Africans feel comfortable in their bodies, and I believe that this is just as legitimate a way to Christ as our "head way." Many Asians feel very comfortable in their gut, and that too is a very good way to find God. Latins are often localized in the heart.

We're learning today from these people that in the future the Gospel will be expounded more from the perspective of the body, the heart, or the gut, and less from the head. That doesn't mean that what we've done is wrong. I repeat: the question is not whether we were right or wrong. But this development shows that we're only parts of the whole.

The Christian Church is finally becoming a universal, global Church. This is my hope: I hope in the coming of the cosmic Christ, a Christ whom we comprehend not just in cerebral categories. Back home in New Mexico the Indians dance on their feast days from morning to night. And they ask: "Why isn't this just as good as your praying with your mouth?" I know they're right, of course. And when I see the fruits of their life, I sometimes have the impression that they're "righter" than we are.

Q. *What does the renunciation of being right mean for our relations with our religions?*

A. First of all, I believe we have to commit ourselves to the path to which God has called us. And we have to go all the way along that path. Those of us who have met Christ have to let him lead us all the way. I personally believe that Christ represents most perfectly the heart of God. The Second Vatican Council says that there is the Word of God, namely Christ, but that doesn't mean that there aren't *other* words of God. Our task as Christians is to follow the Word of Christ to the end. Nevertheless this Word of God describes himself as a lamb: That isn't the way of the conqueror, but the way of the victim. The way of Christ is not the way of power, but of powerlessness. We don't run around shouting, "We have the whole truth!" We dedicate our lives as Christ did to be a bridge for reconciliation, as a bridge between those who hate, who fear, who distrust.

Jesus is a person and at the same time a process. Jesus is the Son of God, but at the same time he is "a Way." He's the goal, but he's also the means, and the means is always the way of the cross, which therefore looks altogether different. The way of the cross looks like the way of failure and coming to grief — and that's why faith is so rare. That's why Paul talks about the *folly of the cross*. Too many Christians want nothing except to prove that they've got the true religion. But genuine Christians are concerned with doing what Jesus did. They want to imitate Jesus. And they leave the final judgment to God.

Q. *You say that faith has nothing to do with feelings. But I notice that I have to experience more feelings just to get to action. I think I would prefer to live emotionally and that this is my way of coming to the truth.*

A. I don't mean an either-or, I always mean both-and. Most of us need an emotional experience just to get out of the starting blocks. Precisely because our faith was up in our heads for so long, many of us have to experience the love of God emotionally. Many people have had this experience in the charismatic movement. Feelings are admittedly a good point of departure, but not a good means of continuing to grow spiritually.

I'd like to compare it to a marriage. You can't stretch out the honeymoon forever. If we try to stay on the honeymoon, then we're not in love with a person, but with an idea, with an ideal image. All the great believers that I know are people who surely have moments now and again when they've found deep emotional consolation. But they don't need these moments — and they don't continually run after them. Feelings are a very good thing, but please don't make an idol out of them and don't believe that religion means producing the maximum amount of good feelings. If you do, you remain very immature.

Q. *I don't mean only the good feelings, but the bad feelings too, the ones I have to confront.*

A. That's right. Many of us have been taught to repress negative feelings. That's why I asked you before to allow, feel, and observe your feelings — including the negative ones. Because negative feelings have the power to open us up to parts of ourselves that are still afraid, that can't trust. As long as you haven't become aware of these feelings, you also can't open yourself to God. Otherwise you don't even know who you are. Sometimes you also have to say to God: I'm afraid, or I'm furious, or I feel rejected. The great prayers of all time had the freedom to get furious with God. Job is an example of this.

Q. *When you said that it's important to get together with a person who is completely different from you, I first noticed what a tremendous opportunity lies in marriage. Above all, to persevere after the honeymoon with a person who is just that, completely different.*

A. That's the reason I think almost all people are called to marriage. Because we need another person to be like a mirror for us, to reflect our best self and our worst self. The interesting thing about a mirror is that it doesn't change the image, but simply takes it in as it is. We all need the experience of being loved unconditionally. Without a human experience of unconditional love, which we hope to experience in marriage, we can't believe in God's unconditional love. And this is obviously the case, because to go the whole way with God, we must at the same time go the whole way with another person, though often that's very difficult. For this person always shows us our dark side and reminds us that we still haven't really *learned to love*.

I would like to say once more that I feel it is a great privilege to be here this evening, and that I know that as someone who comes from a completely different country, I'm sure that I've gotten many things wrong. I hope that you yourselves can fill in the gaps. There are only a few people on this globe who have gone through what you have gone through. The older ones among you have been in your lifetime the victims of two terrible ideologies, first from the right and then from the left. But this means that you have a unique chance to learn wisdom. You know that you need a deeper place when you seek for truth. You know now that no party, whether left or right, can offer you the Reign of God.

5   Contemplation — the Spiritual Challenge

I DON'T BELIEVE THAT JESUS had a plan of what the perfect society was supposed to look like. In any case this plan isn't evident from the New Testament. Instead, Jesus gave us a process, a way of hearing, a way of union, a way enabling us to look behind the world of appearances and to press forward to the truth. To be free and empty of oneself, the freedom not to make an idol of any system, that's real freedom that makes community possible.

This evening let's take that journey into emptiness one step further. I call this the journey into contemplation. We live in a society that's highly dependent upon our earning what we're worth. We continually have to find an opportunity to tell ourselves that we're valuable. We do this, for example, with our clothes or with the car we drive. But we have great difficulties finding our value from within. In a materialistic society we have projected our sense of worth almost exclusively onto things. That is why it's hard to rediscover your soul in yourself. I warn you: In a capitalistic society it's much more dangerous than in the one that used to rule the GDR.

People living under capitalism find it very hard to know

A talk given in the Church of the Cross, March 15, 1990.

their own center or to live from within it. We live in an affluent society that's always expecting more, wanting more, and finally believes it has more coming to it. But the more we own, comically enough, the less we enjoy. This is the paradox that lies within all material goods. The more we project our soul's longing onto things, the more things disappoint us, and the less time we have too.

In America people possess many things that they call time-saving conveniences, and yet they run around and never have time. In an affluent society where the soul's longing is projected outward, we have much more information, but much less wisdom. Wisdom means dealing rightly with the information, but information has become a consumer item in its own right. We have no place deep inside us to bring this information to, so we can integrate it there and transform it into wisdom. Hence our social system may produce many specialists, but very few wise men and women. And in the end we're short of knowledge, wisdom, and time.

When the soul is projected outward, we have less time for love, because other people turn into articles for consumption too. We keep asking only: What can this person do for me? How can the other be useful to me? How can this person enrich my own self-image? How can you contribute to making me feel still stronger? That's why there are so few experiences of genuine friendship that's grounded in itself, with no goal above and beyond the relationship. It's also no surprise that we no longer have any notion of the spiritual life, because even God has become a consumer item. In America there are bumper stickers with the slogan, "I found it," with the "it" supposedly standing for God. But actually the "I" stands in the center, *I* found it; even God has become a possession of my ego.

Ultimately we do the same thing to our own souls: We stand, as it were, outside ourselves and pass judgment on ourselves. Are we valuable or aren't we? Are we right or wrong? But as soon as we judge ourselves, we also tear ourselves apart. We chop ourselves up into the part that passes judgment and the part that gets judged. We have to find a way to bring all that back together again. The only way I know is the way of contemplation, which is the total opposite of the way of capitalism. I warn you, before you make your choice in the next days and months: Don't change yourselves unless you know first what you're choosing. Once you've decided for a specific road, it's very hard to turn around.

Jesus quite definitely wanted us to build a society in which people and not things come first. Jesus taught us to love people and to use things. But in our society we use people and love things. Some years ago I was preaching in Africa, in the cathedral of Nairobi. The people listened to me for hours, and in the end they said, Now let's pray together. They trooped into the sanctuary and sat down on the floor. An old black man prayed, "Lord, never let us move into stone houses." And I nodded and said, "Yes, Lord," though I had no idea what this prayer actually meant. The praying lasted more than an hour. Then I went into the sacristy and asked the priest why the man had said this prayer. The priest answered, "You know Africa, you've seen our country. People here live in little huts, and huts have no doors. That's why your family is my family, and my family is your family. The only family is the extended family. But as soon as you move into a stone house, you build a door. And on the door you put a lock. And behind this door you begin to collect your belongings, and then you have to spend the rest of your life defending those belongings." The world is divided for all time into "mine" and "thine."

Over eight hundred years ago Francis of Assisi said exactly the same thing: We own nothing; we're owned by our possessions. I believe this is unavoidable unless we find the place for our soul. If we don't live from within our own center, then we'll go spinning around things. The true goal of all religions is to lead us back to the place where everything is one, to the experience of radical unity with all of humanity and hence to the experience of unity with God. Religion has no other purpose than to make possible this one journey. And this is just what I'd like to describe in somewhat greater detail this evening. But I have to say right off that it's quite difficult to describe this journey with words. For the crucial point is that it's *your* personal journey, a journey that you have to take yourself.

Four years ago my Franciscan superiors gave me a year's leave to spend in contemplation. I know it was a great privilege, and it struck me as a luxury. Perhaps I can pass along to you some of my experiences so that you too can share in them. As a motto for this "sabbatical" I chose the maxim of the Austrian philosopher Ludwig Wittgenstein, "Don't think, Just look." That's why I decided to fast from books, radio, and TV, that is, not to take in any more information and ideas. I wanted to try to get a good clear look at what I had already experienced and lived until then. I didn't need any fresh information; I had to learn to reflect upon previous experiences, to chew them thoroughly. I had to taste on my tongue their positive and their negative sides, their sweetness and their bitterness.

I had previously given a retreat for a Trappist monastery, where the abbot asked me whether he could do me a favor. I asked him to be allowed to live for thirty days in the hermitage of the famous poet-monk Thomas Merton, who died in 1968. I had read the books of Thomas Merton — who was also the teacher of Ernesto Cardenal — and was very enthusiastic about him; he was my model. I thought that if I were at his place, I might be able to incorporate some of his wisdom. And so I managed to spend the spring in the hills of Kentucky, absolutely alone with myself, with the woods, and, I hoped, with God. I thought beforehand that it would probably be deadly boring. I wondered what I'd do all day long. I put my chair in front of the door and watched the sun come up in the morning. And in the late afternoon I placed my chair on the other side of the hut and watched the sun go down.

That doesn't sound especially edifying. I tried to keep a diary of what was happening to me. Because I'm a man and because I'm of German extraction, I find it particularly hard to cry. But one evening I laid my finger on my cheek and found to my surprise that it was wet. I wondered what those tears meant. What was I crying for? I wasn't consciously sad at all or consciously happy. I noticed at this moment that behind it all there was a joy, deeper than any personal joy. It was a joy in the face of the beauty of being. A joy at all the wonderful and lovable people I had already met in my life.

But at the same moment I experienced the exactly opposite emotion. I hadn't known before that two such contrary feelings could coexist. Because the tears were at the same time tears of an immense sadness, a sadness at what we're doing to the earth, sadness at the people whom I have already hurt in my life, and a sadness too at my own emptiness and stupidity. And even today, five years after this experience I still don't know whether joy or pain had the upper hand — both lay so close to one another.

In this year of contemplation I wasn't preaching or teaching anything. I wasn't capable of verbally transmitting my inner truth, and that's why it had to come out of my eyes. There is still another way of knowledge beside the one that passes through the brain, and this is the way of contemplation. Contemplation is a kind of knowledge that the saints called unknowing. They describe it as an encounter with the "cloud of unknowing," where we are no longer governed by the compulsive need for security, where we no longer have to understand everything, where we can say from the depths of our heart: "It's all right." (Although at the same time we know that much is not all right, that many things in the world are terrible.) And nevertheless we find the inner strength to live with reality as it really is.

The best definition for contemplation that I know runs as follows: *Contemplation is a long, loving look at what really is.* The essential element in this experience is time. There is a qualitative difference between ten minutes and ten hours, and all the more, of course, between ten hours and ten days. We have to find a place where we can receive all our experiences without repressing anything. We need a place where there's room for everything that we've done — and not done — in our life, a place that's bigger than Yes or No, a place bigger than the judgments that we pass. At this all-embracing place God becomes quite clear. Here there is room for every part of you.

Some years ago I gave a Bible course on the subject of redemption. We went through the whole Bible and looked at how the theme of redemption, of salvation, unfolds. The first presentation of salvation is the promise that God gives to the people of Israel. God promises to give them a spacious country to wrap them round. When we had gone through the whole Bible, we could find no better description of redemption than this first one: God promises us a spacious place within — and that's the place we call the soul. We don't *save* our soul, we *discover* it. We don't go there and try to make ourselves holy, we wake our souls up. We're already united with God; the problem is, we don't believe it.

This is the question of faith, but we've turned it into a question of our worthiness. That's exactly what capitalism makes out of the Gospel: We turn everything into an earned value. We can't understand grace. We can't understand love. We can't believe that we're loved for nothing, absolutely nothing. Our real value depends on what we are and not what we do. We continually try to be good people, whatever that means. In reality we are not always *good*, but we are *holy*. Being good is something that you earn or acquire or achieve, but we're holy because we came forth from God. That's just a fact.

Contemplation means that we return to this deep source. Each one of us has to try to find the spiritual exercise that helps us to come to this source. If reading the Bible helps you, then read the Bible. If the Eucharist helps, then celebrate the Eucharist. If praying the rosary helps, pray the rosary. If sitting in silence helps, just sit there and keep silence. But we must find a way to get to the place where everything is. We have to find this long, loving look at reality, where we don't judge any more, where we simply receive.

Most of us have lived our whole life long with a permanent stream of consciousness, with a continual flow of ideas, images, and feelings. And at every moment of our lives we cling to such ideas or feelings. That's why the following happens: I don't have the idea, the idea has me. I don't have a feeling, the feeling has me. We have to dis-

cover who this *I* really is, the one who has these feelings
or these thoughts. Who are you yourself — behind your
thoughts and feelings?

I'm sure that most people in the Western world have
never really met the person who they themselves are. Because at every moment all our life long we identify ourselves either with our thoughts, our self-image, or with our
feelings. We have to find a way to get behind our thoughts,
feelings, and self-image. We have to discover the face that
we already had before we were born. We have to find out
who we were all along in God before we did anything right
or wrong. This is the first goal of contemplation.

I ask you to imagine a river or stream. You're sitting on
the bank of this river, where boats and ships are sailing.
While the stream flows past your inner eye, I ask you to
name each one of these boats and ships. For example, one
of the boats could be called "my anxiety about tomorrow."
Or along comes the ship "objections to my husband," or
the boat "Oh, I don't do that well." Every judgment that
you pass is one of those boats. Take the time to give each
one of them a name, and then let it move on.

For some people this is a very difficult exercise, because
we're used to jumping aboard the boats immediately. As
soon as we own a boat, and identify with it, it picks up
energy. But what we have to practice is non-possessing,
letting go. With every idea, with every image that comes
into our head we say, "No, I'm not that; I don't need that;
that's not me." Again and again we have to tell ourselves
this. Some of the boats that are already used to our jumping aboard them immediately think we just didn't see them
the first time. That's why they head back upstream and return. The boat says: "But before this he always used to get
mad at his wife. Why didn't he this time?" Some of you

will feel the need to torpedo your boats. But don't do it, please don't attack these boats. Don't hate them or condemn them: This is also an exercise in non-violence. You aren't allowed to hate your soul, you can't hate your soul. The point is to recognize things and to say: That's not necessary, I don't need that. But do it very amiably. If we learn to handle our own souls tenderly and lovingly, then we'll be able to carry this same loving wisdom into the world outside.

Many of us have come to know only a totalitarian spirituality. For this reason it's also no surprise that we have produced two totalitarian worldviews: capitalism and communism. Both are lies. We have to learn the truth, not in our head, but in our soul, at the place where great freedom is, where God is patient and accepts everything, and where we must learn to accept everything too. At the same time, we aren't allowed to remain stuck to anything. This is also an exercise in letting go. Positive thoughts are just as bad as negative thoughts, positive feelings are just as bad as negative feelings — if we get attached to them. Positive self-images are just as addictive as negative self-images — if we cling to them. That's why Jesus says: Blessed are the poor in spirit. The poor are the ones who don't hang on to any image that they have of themselves, who don't have to punish themselves with negative images, but also who don't continually have to protect their positive self-images.

Psychology can only help us to arrange our images somewhat differently, to get a somewhat more positive image of ourselves. But authentic spirituality not only shifts the images, it says, "I don't need any images at all, I don't have to protect any self-image." If you see this exercise through, in a short time you'll know which images you personally cling to, which patterns of thought give you your energy. I warn you, it's a humiliating experience at first. Because most people will find out that they don't know who they are, apart from their thoughts and feelings. But after only a few minutes some will find that the river is cleared of boats. Occasionally it even happens that people have the feeling that they'd love to tear their clothes off and dive into the river: the water is our spiritual self that flows much deeper than our psyche.

St. Bonaventure says, "Being and goodness are one and the same thing." That's why we have to return to the level where we simply "are," where we're naked, and where we experience how "good" we are. But this goodness has no relation to doing something correctly or incorrectly. We have to return to this place; otherwise there will never be any radical reformation of religion, nor will there be any really new politics. Otherwise there will only be one ego warring against another. An ego with a right-wing ideology is just as bad as an ego with a left-wing ideology. A conservative ego is just as bad as a liberal ego. A capitalist ego is just as bad as a communist ego. Genuine religion leads us beyond these ego-centric attitudes and helps us to see who we are in God. There we have the freedom to be poor and ordinary. We don't have to prove anything, we don't have to defend anything; and we return from this place to the world with greater strength. Indeed we're flung back into the world.

After my sabbatical year I found my way to the conviction that I should open the Center for Action and Contemplation in New Mexico to help people to get thoroughly involved in the issues and goals of social justice, to help people really turn to the poor, but from the right point of departure (because you can do the right thing for wrong reasons). For this reason I ask you now simply to sit in silence for six minutes. Please think about this: With this exercise there's no such thing as success or failure. The important thing is to see it through and to keep letting go of the unnecessary false self — and not to be afraid.

Because being and goodness are identical. The goal of all spirituality is that in the end the naked person stands before the naked God. The important thing is that we're naked. As you know, the act of love requires nakedness. And the same is true with loving God. We have to cast off our false self to be ready for real unity with God. Don't be afraid of the silence, because God is with you and leading you in that silence.

After the exercise you should take a few minutes' and try to find a word, an adjective, a phrase for what happened ("false" or "correct" does not apply here) to you during these six minutes. Even if it frightened you, or if you had the feeling that you couldn't do it, share that. And if it was wonderful and peaceful, then share that. I ask you simply to turn to a few people around you and try to share this little experience with one another, even though you may have found it difficult. Take a few minutes for this. Contemplation is a way to hear with the Spirit and not with the head. Contemplation is the search for a wide-open space. This space is broad enough for the head to have room in it, it's broad enough for the heart, the feelings, the gut, the subconscious, our memories, our intuitions, for our whole body. We need a holistic place for hearing. Christians have to go to this place if they're looking for wisdom. If we don't produce any more wise men and women, then the reason is that we have forgotten the art of contemplation.

QUESTIONS and ANSWERS

Q. *As soon as I go back to normal life, I don't recall a whole lot from my silent time. But contemplation has to have consequences for my daily life. How can I manage to live with those "boats" in the everyday scene?*

A. Your question is extremely important. Of course, we have to return to our boats, but I can't have any genuine freedom unless I know who I am apart from this boat. In the final analysis the purpose of letting go is so that I can really and freely lay hold of something. And the purpose of this new liberation from bondage is so I can commit myself from free and healthy motives. The effect of contemplation is authentic action, and if contemplation doesn't lead to genuine action, then it remains pure navel-gazing and self-preoccupation.

But I'm convinced that if you stick with it, if you do this exercise regularly, then you'll come to the inner place of compassion. In this place you'll notice how much the suffering of the world is your suffering, and how committed you are to this world, not cerebrally, but from the much stronger perspective of your soul. At this point you're indestructible, because there you find the peace that the world cannot give. You don't need to win anymore; you just need to do what you have to do. Because you're doing it not from an ego-centric place, but from a soul-centric place. That's why Paul can say: "Although I have been whipped, although I have suffered shipwreck, none of that can stop me" (2 Cor. 11:25).

Paul found the source of his strength at a deeper place than in his head. But you can't solve the problem by just acting "interiorly" or from correct inner motives. I also suggest committing oneself in solidarity to a person who is different from you or me, for example, to an old person, a handicapped person, a retarded person, a homosexual or a person on welfare. If we view reality from the standpoint of others, then we'll experience complete conversion, namely inner *and* outer transformation. We have "turned around," and that is the biblical meaning of metanoia.

Q. *Thus far you haven't said anything at all about Jesus Christ.*

A. On the way to contemplation we do the same thing that Jesus Christ did in the wilderness. Jesus teaches us not to say, "Lord, Lord," but to do the will of his Father. What must primarily concern us is that we do what Jesus has bidden us do. Jesus went into the wilderness, ate nothing for forty days, and made himself empty. Another image of that emptiness is the body of Mary. She can receive Jesus into that emptiness and bear Christ to the world because she is his poor handmaid.

Q. *I think emptiness isn't enough.*

A. Of course, you're right. Emptiness in and of itself isn't enough. The point of emptiness is that we get ourselves out of the way, so that Christ can fill us up. All I've taught here are the first stages, the fundamentals. Jesus takes it from there!

Q. *How do we come to the love of Christ?*

A. First, we don't choose Christ. Christ chooses us, he decides for us. As soon as we're empty, there's a place for Christ, because only then are we in any sense ready to recognize and accept Christ as the totally other, who is not me.

Q. *After weeks of exercise I have experienced this emptiness, I can now let go of everything. What's the next step? Isn't there a danger of doing something wrong? How can you find your true identity after you've dropped the false and evil identity?*

A. Our goal consists in doing the will of the Father in heaven. Thus we first have to remove our attachment to our own will, so that we can recognize the difference between the two. Many people who did horrible things were unshakably convinced that they were doing the will of God. That's why we have to find an instrument to distinguish between God and us. Paul calls this the gift of discernment of spirits. We have to learn when my own spirit is at work and when the Spirit of God is at work. This exercise is only a very rudimentary little step toward contemplation. I'm sure there are a thousand further steps.

Q. *This exercise was a wonderful thing. If you look at these inner images, you learn a great deal about yourself. If you do this spiritual exercise, you find your own reality. I've never had an experience that helped me so much to find my reality.*

A. I'd like to encourage you to keep on going. If this exercise teaches you nothing, then please try something else. The only person who prays well is the one who prays often. The only success (if you want to talk about success in this context) is success in sticking to it, in hanging on. With emptiness we are, so to speak, cultivating a good land where we can be receptive to the seed of God's word. Once again, I don't believe that Jesus dumps the harvest into our lap. He shows us a process of growth. He shows us a way we can learn to hear God. He shows us a way we can forgive. He shows us a way of self-surrender. He trusts that his people, as they go along this way, will learn to hear the truth ever more clearly. The great truth will always lie beyond us. The great truth will never underpin a small world.

The most convincing social activists in our country were and are at the same time people of prayer: men and women like Dorothy Day, Martin Luther King, or Jim Wallis. It's very important that we bring these two groups together in the Church: the contemplatives and the activists. Because neither is credible without the other. Both incorporate only a half of Christ. Christ went into the wilderness for forty days; only after that did he begin to preach the Reign of God and to heal the sick. And along the way he kept saying to his disciples: "Come, let us withdraw and find a quiet, peaceful place" (see Matt. 14:23).

This means that our whole Christian life must be a constant back and forth between the radical way inward and the radical way outward. We all begin either on one side or the other. That's why we all have to be converted so that we come to the place where both meet. In the GDR you have an enormous opportunity of becoming a wise people, precisely because you have gone through so much that people in other countries have not. I beg you, take the narrow path of wisdom. It's not a path that the politicians, whether on the right or the left, can understand; but it's the path of the true Church and the way of Christ.

6   The Freedom
of the Sons and Daughters
of God (Luke 8)

I N MY BOOK *Der wilde Mann* (The wild man) I tried to describe how men can be liberated. In *Der nackte Gott* (The naked God) I spoke about how the Church might be freer. In *Discovering the Enneagram* Andreas Ebert and I describe how individual men and women can become free. And on Sunday Christa Mulack will perhaps help me explain how women can become free. Needless to say, that's not my job.

Freedom is certainly a subject that has greatly moved you all in the last few months. I just got back from Dresden, where your brothers and sisters still have a lot of even more serious grappling to do with this question. It's important for them that in the next few days they reach a decision for freedom, for real freedom.

I'd like to read you a couple of sentences that I wrote in my diary only an hour ago: "The difference between a country in the Second World (East Germany) and a country in the First World (West Germany) is shocking. But the difference shocks you in a different way than the difference between a Third World and a First World country. For decades the East has been totally dominated and controlled,

A talk given in Holy Spirit Hall, Nuremberg, March 16, 1990.

intellectually and emotionally; and all this happened within the borders of one and the same nation. Yet what an illustration Germany is of the power of a different social contract, of the power of a different culture and social order to transform our thinking. In the East it looks as if people had internalized the passivity that was permanently demanded of them. This affected their work ethic, their motivation, their proverbial German cleanliness, and many other features of their life. We always thought that these were inalterable German virtues, but circumstances have forced even the industrious Germans to go in a different direction."

Here in the West meanwhile, in Nuremberg, you've been able to cultivate those virtues, but that meant primarily private, individual interests. Is there really no way to move individuals to seek the common good of their own accord? Of their own accord! Is that the exclusive, thankless task of the Church? Is that the Church's never-ending responsibility? The world isn't capable of recognizing genuine freedom or of making it possible. It doesn't even have the tools for the job. Besides, the world necessarily operates on the basis of particular interests, and so private egoism is simply extended through group egoism.

For me this is exactly the situation that we have to deal with: How can we, as men and women of the Church, really be liberated? How can we pass on this freedom to the world? I would like to clarify this question on the basis of a story (from Luke 8) about a miraculous cure.

> Then they arrived at the country of the Gerasenes, which is opposite Galilee. And as he stepped out on land, there met him a man from the city who had demons; for a long time he had worn no clothes, and he lived not in a house but among the tombs.

This is a picture of a man who lives among the dead and isn't quite civilized, because he runs around naked. We shall soon see that the city feels just fine about the fact that this man lives out there — and so does he. Because when Jesus comes to him, we are told:

> When he saw Jesus, he cried out and fell down before him, and said in a loud voice: "What have you to do with me, Jesus, Son of the Most High God? I beseech you, do not torment me."

That means, I don't know whether I want what you have. The unfreedom I have is the only world I know.

We feel much more comfortable with our slavery than with freedom. Freedom means that we have to assume radical responsibility for what we are. To be enslaved means that we always have somebody else to blame for our problems. The spirit had already possessed this man for a long time: "He was bound with chains and fetters." In this way people tried to keep him under control. Although they kept him chained, they said the evil spirit was holding him captive. When we project the darkness in us onto another person or other groups, then these people or groups end up accepting our projection. Sooner or later we all believe the world's version of who we are. Hitherto we've always tried to realize freedom as the liberation of specific individuals. But Western Christianity has for the most part neglected to address the problem of institutional evil and structural sin. Christianity has often not recognized that in a great number of cases such evil is the primary cause of our individual unfreedom. And we shall see how true that is, if we go on reading the story.

"Jesus then asked him, 'What is your name?' and he said, 'Legion.'" This means that evil has many faces, and it's hard to give it a concrete name. It's very hard to pigeonhole this evil, because many demons had entered the man, and he had been told many lies.

And the demons begged him not to command him to depart into the abyss. Now a large herd of swine was feeding there on the hillside; and they begged him to let them enter these.

(On the question of why evil has such a strong impulse toward bodies, see M. Scott Peck, *The People of the Lie* [New York: Simon & Schuster, 1983].) The herd of swine naturally stands for the economy of this region: The people of this region were keeping their economic heads above water by raising pigs.

So he gave them leave. Then the demons came out of the man and entered the swine, and the herd rushed down the steep bank into the lake and were drowned. When the herdsmen saw what had happened, they fled, and told it in the city and the country. Then the people went out to see what had happened, and they came to Jesus, and found the man from whom the demons had gone, sitting at the feet of Jesus, clothed, and in his right mind.

You would expect the next line to say, "And they all rejoiced," or "They were very happy." But verse 35 says, "and they were afraid."

Back home in America we work with broken and alcoholic families. We often find that the whole family dances around the one sick person and gets upset about how terrible this sick person is and how hard family life is because of this sick person. But as soon as the alcoholic decides to get healthy, nobody gets more agitated about it than this family. Because now they no longer have anyone to shame or blame; now they have to grow up themselves. We call this co-dependency. We reciprocally bind one another with our lies; we bind one another through our negative feelings and our negative ways of thinking. And this holds true not just for families, but also for churches, for institutions, and for countries. Moving away from this death trap always brings us a terrible amount of anxiety. That's why, for example, Jesus says something that we've never understood. He says we must dare to hate "father and mother and brother and sister" (Luke 14:26). Preachers hesitate to give a sermon on this text because we don't know how to handle it. He says that the family and society can be a source of death, just as they can be a source of life.

The eyewitnesses report how this man was healed. And then the whole crowd of people from the region of Gerasa begs Jesus to leave their territory. The whole city says: "Get out of here, you've ruined our economy. Our pigs are dearer to us than salvation, because our pigs are our source of income. We can't imagine that our economy also ruins us; our economic system is our salvation, not you."

The practical definition of freedom that we have under capitalism runs as follows: It's the freedom to have endless possibilities and options. Ronald Reagan once told us that America was a great and free nation because we can choose from thirty-nine flavors of ice cream. And we make such people heads of state! But Jesus also said that we should expect no wisdom from the world. The freedom it offers us is always a freedom that serves its own purposes. It is a tiny freedom. It is the Pax Romana, not the Pax Christi.

"Then the man from whom the demons had gone begged that he might join him." We meet here one "born-again," someone who has just experienced a cure and who would like to deepen his personal relationship with Jesus.

He'd like things to be "warm and cozy" between himself and Jesus. "But Jesus sent him away, saying, 'Return to your home, and declare how much God has done for you.' " Because you're no longer the problem, the people in the city are! And it makes no sense at all for me to liberate people and evangelize them and send them back into sick cities, send them back into sick countries, while at the same time they can have their private little freedom with the Lord Jesus.

Individualism has taken away the credibility of the Gospel in the Western world because we think we can seek our private freedom — independently of others. Genuine evangelization must move forward on two rails at the same time. We must simultaneously evangelize individuals and call them to freedom *and* evangelize institutions, nations, and systems, calling them to conversion. If you do the first, everyone will call you a saint, if you do the second, you'll be called a communist and a revolutionary. And for this reason most of us remain on the safe first side. None of us is ready for the full freedom of Christ. We want the freedom of Christ only so long as they don't take our "swine" away from us, and we can live comfortably "among the tombs."

Anne Wilson Schaef has published a very helpful book in which she deals with our personal addictions and dependencies; she describes Western society as a dependent society (*When Society Becomes an Addict* [San Francisco: Harper & Row, 1987]). The obvious dependencies are, of course, alcohol, nicotine, coffee, food. In America the so-called Twelve Step programs are doing a booming business. Everybody belongs to one self-help group or another. And these groups are growing five times as fast as any born-again Church. There are "Gamblers Anonymous," "Overeaters Anonymous," "Neurotics Anonymous," "Fundamentalists Anonymous," and "Cowards Anonymous." But we have discovered a second kind of unfreedom and addictive dependency and call them "process addictions."

It's quite clear that the accumulation, the collecting and saving of money, is an addiction. People pile up so much money that they can't spend it in a lifetime. Yet some of these people have the nerve to quote the Sermon on the Mount and consider themselves followers of the poor Jesus. There are also workaholism and the addiction to buying things — both process addictions. In America they say, "Shop till you drop." People buy things as a pastime, as recreation. Germany too has its fair share of department stores full of things nobody needs. We have little boutiques that sell only pink soap, and we think we need this wonderful pretty pink soap — and a matching soap tray.

Twenty-eight years ago I was a novice in the Franciscans, and back then we were told a great deal about letting go. We were taught that less is more, and that the thing for Franciscans was to live simply in this world. For many years now people in our order have scarcely been talking any more about letting go. But if you can't talk about letting go, you're already an addict. If you forget the virtue of giving away, of letting go, you're already an addict.

All spirituality is about letting go. How to let go of our security, how to let go of our good reputation, how to let go of our identity and our self-image. All great contemplative teachers lead us in this direction. But because we no longer understand any of this, we have become an addictive society and an addictive Church. A large part of religion shows all the indications of addiction and dependency. People who are turned on by a certain kind of language and by a desperate attempt to maintain their self-image, people, for example, who need to consider themselves good or redeemed. They run to Jesus and say, "Good master," and his answer is, "Why do you call me good?" (Mark 10:8).

Jesus doesn't use religion to defend his self-image. A large part of religion is the attempt to maintain one's own self-image; but this is not a genuine search for God. But we can't find God alone; God finds us. All that we can learn is how to let go. And there also we have to pray: "Lord, show me how I can let go."

For Anne Wilson Schaef there is *one* addiction that over-arches all these quite private addictions and dependencies: Our chief addiction is *addiction to the system itself.* Our chief dependency is the dependency on our hallowed explanations. Could there be a world not built on competition? We can't imagine it. And that shows how dependent on the system we are. Could there be a world not built on power? We can't imagine it. Which shows how dependent we are. Could there be a world not built on money and control? Could there be a world not built on militarism? We have to throw the Sermon on the Mount out the window, because judged from the viewpoint of other explanations of the world we're all addicts.

In her first book Schaef still cautiously called the system "the white male system" (naturally that prompted many furious letters to her from white males). That is why she says in her second book, "I no longer call it 'the white male system,' I now call it 'the addictive system.'" But it's white men who in the first instance profit from it. It's white men who in the first instance have laid down the rules for it. This system works to their advantage. And I have to say that because I am a white man. I come from a country that considers itself the best country in the world. I belong to the gender that considers itself more powerful and intelligent than the opposite sex. I have spent many years going through the educational system. I am an ordained priest. That means, I stand right at the top of the pyramid.

Often the thought goes through my head: How can I really understand the Gospel at all? Because the Gospel — as Francis of Assisi illustrates — is best understood when you're below and not when you're on top. It's precisely for this reason that I have an unfair advantage, why I'm under a compulsion to speak. If a woman got up to say the same thing, she'd be called a raging feminist. If a layman stood up, they'd say he must have had bad experiences with the clergy. If somebody from another country said it, they'd say, he's just anti-American or anti-capitalistic. That's why *I* have to say it. I enjoy the fruits of the system. It was created for me and my kind.

Schaef goes on to say that the addictive system is undergirded by five myths. Until we look these five myths in the eye, we haven't begun to become free from society, because we're dependent upon a lot of social props that we don't recognize or admit to.

The first myth runs as follows: There is only the male system. Our worldview is the only rational way to look at reality. All fairly intelligent and clever people think exactly this way. But the Gospel says that until we leave behind our own standpoint, we are not yet converted. It's called narcissism or cultural arrogance. The biblical word for it is "blindness." Jesus, for example, never suggests that rich people are deliberately bad or mean. He says they're merely blind, they can't see. The rich man can't see that Lazarus is eating the crumbs in front of his door. He even leaves him the crumbs (Luke 16:19ff.). He's a charitable person, but he understands nothing of justice. The great question in the spiritual life is always the question of blindness and sight. And therefore our prayer must always be, "Lord, help me to see. Let me see where the demons really are — and what the village really loves."

The second myth maintains that this system, our way of thinking and living, is by nature superior to all other ways and hence its rules and laws have to be binding for everyone. America, for example, wants to arm the world for democracy. And should elections not turn out to our satisfaction, then we decide on a trade embargo against the country and send money to influence the next election. And when the election works out the way we want it, then we triumphantly rejoice over the "victory of democracy."

The third myth consists in thinking that our system is omniscient, that our way of thinking and living gives us the right to judge the reality of other people. White men know what the poor need. White men know what blacks need. White men know what women need. With that sort of attitude there's obviously no possibility of a turnaround and change. And that's why in this context "conversion" is understood as something very private, limited, individual, or sacramental. I can have my intimate relationship with the Lord Jesus and dispense with going back to the "village."

The fourth myth claims that because we have the truth, it's possible for us to be absolutely logical, rational, and objective. And whoever doesn't agree with us is simply not intelligent.

And that leads to the fifth and most shocking myth: If the four previous myths are true, we ourselves can be God, because we are almighty and omniscient. But if you take yourself to be God, then you call everybody who criticizes you a devil. Never forget, dear sisters and brothers, that it was the religious people who called Jesus a "devil" (John 8:48). It wasn't the prostitutes, the alcoholics, or the tax-collectors — they didn't call him Beelzebub. It was the good, well-behaved religious people who wanted to safeguard their self-image, who wanted to maintain their theology, who wanted to stabilize their church system.

Sometimes we clerics have the hardest time hearing the Gospel. Sometimes it's very hard for us to speak about freedom, because then you would not need us. Sometimes I believe that what we pastors mainly do is keep our jobs safe. We can't let you stay independent of us. We clerics must finally have the courage to allow you your necessary spiritual path, with all the risks that entails for our church systems. Of course, you'll make mistakes in the process, but we've made them already anyhow. What seduces us into assuming that what we've done until now is so terrific? Choosing the path of freedom always means taking a risk-filled route. It means taking the chance of perhaps doing something wrong. There's always the risk of making mistakes. But what is a mistake? And what does a mistake on the spiritual path mean?

Success has very little to teach us in the spiritual life, but failure and fiascoes are great teachers. Continual experience of so-called conversion teaches us little, while sin is a great instructor. We learn much more from our pains than from our pleasant feelings. We learn much more from letting go than from holding tight. And the task of the Church is to send you off on this journey, where you get to know the truth down in the gut and in the heart and even in the head. Where you know it, as it were, through and through. Now it's not other people's experience or knowledge but your own journey. We cannot take away the responsibility that God gives each person. We can only transmit the experience of our ancestors.

We can trust ourselves to make this personal journey if at the same time we have the freedom to come together as brothers and sisters. If in this community you share your hearts with one another and you try to be honest and searching: "Am I crazy? Am I completely off base?" And if you give your brothers and sisters the right to say, "Yes, you're nuts." If you can ask them, "Do I love Jesus or am I in love with myself?" And if you give them the right to say, "Yes, you're more in love with yourself " — that's the mystery of the Church, that's where the Church becomes concrete.

In 1961 the pope asked us to send 10 percent of our personnel to Latin America. Nobody did it. Even people who claim that they obey the pope didn't do it. When I went to Latin America, I was told: "We're glad they didn't send any priests then. If the priests had come, things would have gone on the way they always had. This doesn't mean that we don't want to celebrate any Eucharists or that we don't want to have God's word preached. But we were forced to seek out our own way, and now we have a country like Brazil with between eighty and a hundred thousand base communities."

It seems to me that Jesus is renewing the Church not from above but from below. The little communities need the large, universal history. Otherwise it can easily happen that they fall into cheap liberalism or narrow New Age thought, into things that have little social force because they once again concentrate on the privatized self. But conversely if we have only the large institution without the radical little group alongside it, then the institution turns into a cold, dead skeleton.

I come from the Franciscan tradition. Francis of Assisi didn't leave the Church as a rebel; very quietly he built a little chapel on the edge of the city. He learned to pray, he learned to surrender himself, he learned to let go. His life spoke out prophetically. Because in the final analysis we live our way into a new kind of thinking, but we in the West have always thought we could think our way into a new way of life. You have to run with your own feet to some place where you haven't been before — to a new place. You have to leave the world where you have everything under control. You have to leave the world where everybody likes you. You have to head into a world where you are poor and powerless. And there you'll be converted despite yourself.

It often happens that the people we went to convert end up by converting us, if we really have the freedom to take up their pain. I think this is what Jesus' healing is all about. Jesus doesn't turn the people into Lutherans or Catholics; he touches their human pain. And people who live among graves suddenly find that through Jesus they have been freed from that pain.

Nothing that I'm saying can be solved by our thinking about it. For twenty years now I've been preaching all over the world — the sermons of priests and pastors convert no one. Just consider how many sermons you've already heard in your life. *Circumstances* convert people! You have to make your way to new circumstances, so that reality can really get to you, because that's where Jesus has hidden himself: in human flesh. Christ always comes into the world on an ass, Christ always comes into the world as a beggar (Mother Teresa calls it "his most distressing disguise"). But we would so much like to have him enclosed in the Church and in our theology. But God is always free.

That's why Jesus says in Matthew 25 that we will be

judged on the basis of only one thing. Jesus defines freedom in an incredibly concrete manner. It has nothing philosophical about it, it has nothing at all to do with conservatism or liberalism, nor with whether you're right or wrong: Either you do it or you don't. He says: "There is only one thing you have to do. You must have the freedom to recognize Christ where you didn't expect him, otherwise you aren't free. And you will be judged on a single question: "Could you recognize Christ in the least of your brothers and sisters?" The people ask, "When did we see you hungry and thirsty and naked?"

Obviously those who did this were not in the least aware that they had met Christ. They didn't do it for Jesus, they simply did it. They didn't even talk about having a personal relationship with Jesus Christ. Please forgive me if this shocks you, but that's what it says in Matthew 25. Of course, I hope you do have a personal relationship with Jesus Christ; but there are people who have no such conscious relationship and nevertheless do Christ's truth. And many of us know the words, but don't do the truth. And then we discover Christ in a place where we never would have guessed he'd be. Until this transformation occurs, we can't call ourselves free. And I'd like to repeat: All this is nothing that we can do; it happens to us. The only thing we can do is get ourselves out of the way. Don't take yourselves too seriously. Let's be empty and open and ready, then Christ himself will be our teacher.

QUESTIONS and ANSWERS

Q. *I was very upset when you presented our economic system without making any distinctions. Do you know any economic system in practice that's more socially conscious than ours? I too can imagine a lot of things being different and better — in Utopia.*

A. It's not as if the capitalistic system has no value of any kind. But the Gospel frees us from making an idol of any system whatsoever. We must have the freedom to see the dark side of capitalism. If I were preaching in another economic system, I'd have to be just as critical; but here you don't need to hear anything from me about the dark side of socialism. The Gospel always has to be preached in a social context — and the one we face in capitalism is different from the one in socialism.

When I read the New Testament, I don't get the impression that Jesus had a concrete plan for society that would go far beyond what I call *non-idolatry* or *letting go.* Jesus frees us from ourselves and from our illusions, so that genuine community becomes possible. But I can never expect any nation-state to understand anything like that. For far too long we have looked to the nation-state for our salvation; that's not its job. In his new encyclical, *Laborem Exercens*, where he speaks about capitalism and communism, the pope says that both are totalitarian systems, both are corrupt, and both exploit the Third World. Although the pope has said that, you don't often hear this viewpoint in the churches. We're used to the Church's saying that socialism is false, but we wouldn't like the Church to uncover the dark side of capitalism. That was my intention here. By doing that I don't want to shame us, but to contribute to our liberation. I'm a "capitalist" too. We have nothing to lose unless we are addicted or at the top of the pile.

Q. *When it comes to liberation, where does that leave women?*

A. We'll explore this subject more deeply on Sunday, so just this much for now: I find it exciting that in our time the Gospel is finally being read through other eyes than just those of white, theologically educated men. And these other eyes come to altogether different insights — with the same Bible that we've been senselessly squabbling over for centuries.

For me there are four important new interpretations of the Bible: The first is to read it through the eyes of *women*. Women normally don't start right off by asking questions about power and control. Second, there's the reading of the Bible through the eyes of the *poor*. At the beginning of this century 70 percent of all Christians lived in North America and Europe. In ten years it will be exactly the reverse: In the year 2000, 70 percent of all Christians will live in the Third World. And therein lies a great hope for the conversion of the Church. The third kind of exposition is through *community*, instead of the endless individualistic interpretations of the prosperous West. I got to know this above all in Africa, but also in other countries, where men and women still think as a group, as a tribe, as a people. For example, their first question is, How can the whole tribe benefit? and not, How can I be saved? With the South Africans you can see that isn't the way they move. They live shoulder to shoulder as you see in their non-choreographed unity. That's an altogether different way of living; communitarian people will read the Gospel in a completely different way. Not "how do I get saved?" as much as "Why are things this way?"

And the fourth new way of seeing is reading the Bible with the eyes of the *mystics*, with the eyes of contemplatives. You find them everywhere in the whole world, but it seems to come most naturally to the people in Asia.

I think the gift that Europe and North America have to offer first of all is biblical interpretation by women. And to some extent in my book *The Wild Man* I try to encourage men to look at their reality through the eyes of women too. Paradoxically this is just what makes them "wild men."

Q. *You said that we get liberated from our selves and that we shouldn't take ourselves too seriously. So far as I've found, God takes me seriously as a person, and therefore I become capable of community. Do you see it differently?*

A. You've put your finger on the paradox. I'm convinced that authentic spirituality is always paradoxical. I even think that any "common sense" that doesn't have a certain paradoxical character deserves to be distrusted. Of course, you are right: God takes me very seriously. But this frees me from the burden of having to do that chore myself. Perhaps it's a problem of semantics, but I can say that I take myself very seriously and at the same time not very seriously at all. And in the same moment both statements are entirely true.

Q. *I liked the fact that you say we're not converted by sermons but by circumstances. But in the Lutheran tradition, now as always, the sermon is the center of Christian life. It's all very well organized, like the way the Church is built up; it's not accidental. Can you tell us how we can change the system,* *how we can live so we have more contact with the poor and the people on the margin?*

A. If as a Catholic I may be allowed to say this, I believe the dark side of Protestantism consists in its being too much the prisoner of the left brain. The pulpit is enthroned as the center of the church's space, to move the *word* of God into the center. This is a good theological concern, but at the same time it has idolized and exalted the left side of the brain. It's given us the impression that we could unite people with words. That's absurd. We'll never all consent to the same words — that's why the Word became flesh. It was not enough for the Word to remain a word, it had to become flesh. And we Christians are still scandalized by the Incarnation. Since 1981 it has been scientifically proved that there are two hemispheres in the brain with two quite different functions. I have to put particular emphasis on this because I'm in Germany. The German-speaking nations are the most strongly influenced by the left half of the brain.

The left brain analyzes reality. It remains in the brain and never goes beyond it. It believes that the knowledge and interpretation of all individual aspects are enough to understand the whole. This worldview sees things as either-or. The left brain can't deal with paradoxes; it can't stand contradictions. The right half of the brain is exactly the opposite. The right brain recognizes reality through synthesis. It argues from its understanding of the whole back to the parts. And it comes to see reality through symbols and images. The right brain is concerned with things like symbols, song, or art. And of course both halves of the brain are "true." But they're true only when they allow the opposite side to be true as well. That's why they're bound together by the corpus callosum. In the last thousand years we have increasingly neglected the right brain. That's the reason for the expansion of the "white male system." This system has an inner logic, which serves to keep the system intact. It's logic is largely left-brain.

Jesus is much more holistic. He speaks and he acts. Then he goes on speaking and goes on acting. He touches, experiences, and lives reality in his body. He goes, for example, to the pagan, non-Jewish world, and lets a Syro-Phoenician woman tell him that he's wrong. He's ready to learn. He has a theology of the flesh.

I believe that the left and right halves of the brain are both wonderful gifts, but only when they work together to lead us to a more holistic view of reality. This is the case when we reach decisions, act, and commit ourselves to quite different positions. It can mean, for instance, that we take a step in solidarity toward the mentally handicapped; or that we involve ourselves with the pain and loneliness of the elderly or with AIDS patients. Somehow or other we have to get out of our own world and make room for the pain of other people. We won't manage this by logical reflection. And our ego will find a thousand excuses why we're not ready for it. But faith means giving away what we thought we didn't even have. That's why it's faith.

Q. *Do you discover your German ancestors when you act this way with the left brain?*

A. Paradoxically, I have to speak from the standpoint of the left hemisphere to help people free themselves from the left hemisphere! Moses held the serpent up in the air for those who had been bitten by serpents. But I grant that I too am a "left-brain" German: That's my gift and my cross. It was important to me, for example, that I've lived in a community with *women and children*, and that I now live in New Mexico with *Indians*. These two experiences have helped me to cross over a little more to the other side.

Q. *Would you also say something about the dark side of Catholicism?*

A. In America I wrote a book called *Why Be Catholic?* (Cincinnati: St. Anthony Messenger Press, 1990).The second chapter is "The Dark Side of Catholicism." Naturally people bought the book just to read the second chapter. I believe that the dark side of Catholicism is its *triumphalism*, an exaggerated fascination with its own past, which was largely European. Although it calls itself "Catholic," i.e., all-embracing, to this day the Catholic Church has in fact remained largely a European Church. The dark side of Catholicism is its refusal to be *really* catholic, to be a really universal Church.

The Catholic Church keeps falling into the trap of social prejudices. And because it has its foundation in Europe, the Catholic Church was very quickly imprisoned in the left half of the brain. In any case it does have an advantage over Protestantism: It has a *past* that was all-embracing and with which it can connect: for example, with the time when the wonderful medieval cathedrals were built, or when there were mystery plays in the church, when the Church knew something about music and art and produced contemplative mystics. But for the most part the Catholic Church has lost all that. But at least it's still present in our memory.

Q. *You've said a lot about freedom and letting go. I see a danger here of taking another path and still winding up back with a people-addiction: to the fairy tale that every individ-*

ual is independent. I believe that Jesus became flesh because he knew precisely that freedom means in the first instance acknowledging our dependence.

A. If I understand you rightly, you're saying something very important. That's why I wanted to say something about the mystery of powerlessness and the mystery of the Church. I believe that one of the reasons why the Twelve Step programs of anonymous groups are so much in demand is that the first step runs something like, "I admit to myself that I'm powerless and incapable of taking my own life in my hands." The teachers of these Twelve Step programs demand from the participants that they hand over their life not only to the whole group (e.g., of other alcoholics) but also to what is called in the programs "a higher power." I would be very disappointed if you interpreted my words as an invitation to individualism. Individualism would engender still more alcoholics. Then I must bear in my own private soul the whole burden of my goodness and my badness. But the teaching of the body of Christ liberates me precisely from this. Society is partially responsible both for my sin and for my virtue. We see this in our biblical story by the way the whole village participates in the imprisonment of an individual, but at the same time the village had the chance to participate in his emancipation.

Q. *What do you mean by conversion through circumstances? For example, in the story of the chained man: He wasn't converted by circumstances, but by Christ.*

A. It's quite clear that in the final analysis it's the grace of Christ that liberates us. It's the experience of unconditional love that really sets us free. But first we have to be led to the circumstances that make it possible for this love to get through to us, so that we can sense and experience the *need* for this new life. I believe that it was precisely the circumstances that converted the man living among the graves. His experience was of being excluded. The pain of always being rejected was what finally made him capable of reaching out to Christ. And that's why Jesus often says that the tax-collectors and the drunkards are more open to the Reign of God than we theologians who have only theories in our heads.

This statement by Jesus is an eternally valid judgment and a warning to us who deal with the Christian faith professionally: It's very dangerous to be a "professional Christian," to be possessed by theories of conversion and salvation. I believe that religion is the safest place to avoid God, because God wants to lead us to self-surrender, and all too often religion teaches us only self-control. And these are two completely different movements: Self-control is a different movement from self-surrender. Genuine self-control is a *fruit* of the Spirit, but it's not the *cause* of the Spirit. Maybe Christ leads us *to* the circumstances and leads us *through* them back to God.

7 What Is This "Women's Stuff"?

Throughout the earth men spoke the same language, with the same vocabulary. But they said to one another, "Come, let us build ourselves a town and a tower with its top reaching heaven." (Gen. 11:1, 4)

In the world the powerful lord it over the others. This must not happen among you. (Luke 22:25–26)

We would probably not have to ask the question in our title if we had understood the lessons in these two Scripture passages. Our title is the question of a male, who is also white, educated, middle-class, and even priestly. Each of these perspectives makes it less likely that I would be aware of "women stuff," much less see any problems or need to change anything. We white males have been holding all the cards, naming all the questions, and providing all the answers for the entire Christian era — except for those few golden years when God took poor flesh in Jesus. He took twelve Jewish men and tried to show them how they could be part of the solution instead of part of the problem. Unfortunately, it didn't work. Males continued to build towers and operate as lords over others, and women

---

A sermon given at a service of biblical commentary in the Church of St. Lawrence, Nuremberg, March 18, 1990; published in this version in *Radical Grace: A Newsletter for the Center for Action and Contemplation*, July–August 1989.

stuff just didn't fit in. That is the world and the Church that I was born into. It is preoccupied with domination and status-quo logic to this day and thus finds itself largely incapable of understanding (much less believing) most of the clear teaching of Jesus. Poverty, meekness or non-violence, tears, justice-love, mercy, purity of heart, peacemaking and reconciliation, bearing persecution or what we might call "losing graciously" are his opening statements. But try to get elected in a Christian country or promoted to a Catholic bishopric today while taking those teachings seriously! Yet Jesus forthrightly called them the Eight Happinesses.

Apparently, Christian men of power have decided that happiness is optional. What is mandatory and necessary is that the world be divided into those who have the power and those who don't. It makes for good order, at least for those on top, and order is more important than happiness. Our word for this addictive view of reality is "patriarchy," which means the "rule of the fathers." It is the basis of all major relational systems in the Western world. In the patriarchal view (1) all relationships are eventually defined in terms of superiority and inferiority, and (2) the all-important need for order and control is assured by the exercise of dominative power. Now that does not sound so bad if the status quo happens to be working in your favor. But it has served to dehumanize and therefore de-spiritualize generations of races, nations, professions, women, sexual minorities, handicapped people, the weak and the elderly whom the powerful are able to disparage culturally and dismiss as "of no account." Not only are the rich and powerful able to project their own darkness onto such groups, but the groups normally accept that darkness as their true value. The utter evil of such patriarchy is that both the oppressor and the oppressed are incapable of real spiritual growth. The powerful, by rejecting their shadow, are hopelessly inflated. The powerless, by receiving others' shadows, are endlessly deflated. Both lose. And that is why patriarchy is evil.

Patriarchy is the nerve center of an entire worldview that idealizes winning over others, power and control (the outer face of fear), and the much abused philosophies of "might makes right" and "peace through strength." Without "success" (by his own definition) and control the patriarch does not know who he is. Many would honestly admit that life would not be worth living, which shows how deep the addiction has become. We must readily admit that many women are also patriarchs in this sense, or at least co-dependent members of the male system. They will often defend it even more feverishly than many males. Witness Margaret Thatcher, Nancy Reagan, and Imelda Marcos!

The language of patriarchy is always a noble or macho language of patriotism and freedom. Men (and their female echoes) are always speaking it, but the amazing thing is that anyone is still willing to believe it. Among other places where it's obviously spoken today are Beirut, Belfast, Moscow, Johannesburg, San Salvador, Washington, and Jerusalem. But fortunately the poor, the oppressed and marginalized, and especially women are beginning to trust their natural and truly religious instincts. In some cases this leads them to mistrust and even disobey the cerebral and self-assured conclusions of the powers that be. You might call that arrogance and pride. You might also call it courage. Or sometimes even faith. God will sort it out; I don't have to. Remember, I'm learning to give up my need for control and explanation!

We have to move toward the instinctual point since left-brain reason and logic have served us so poorly at this point in Western civilization. We find ourselves satisfied with two-thirds of our people either starving, unemployed, or homeless, while unthinkingly polluting and preparing to bomb the rest — and at the same time touting glorious phrases like freedom, free enterprise, "making the world safe for democracy," and "our sacred family values." Man's capacity to disguise his own darkness seems endless. Patriarchal logic is only logic in favor of the system and the status quo — which is proudly called "the real world." Believe me because I always hear it quoted to me after my sermons, usually from polite men in three-piece suits: "That was an interesting talk there, Father, but you know in the real world . . . " The fathers of the system hate nothing more than another father who refuses the rules of the game. That is precisely our role in proclaiming the new system that Jesus called the Reign of God. That's why he trained the twelve men to think and act in a new way. It's sort of a subversion-from-within tactic, but since we have not done very well at it, God is now sending the women to help us.

"Women stuff" is the hidden energy behind almost all the justice issues. The movement toward non-violence and disarmament, the movements that deal with homelessness and refugee problems, with the raping of the earth and its resources, with sexual and physical abuse issues, with the idolatry of profit and the corporation, and with the rejection of the poor will not move beyond the present impasse until the underlying issues of power, prestige, and possessions are exposed for the lie that they are. Under the new Russian perestroika, or "restructuring," we are finally seeing beyond the artificial enemies to the real problem. Surprisingly, we are seeing that the power elites under communism are just as opposed to change as are the wealthy and powerful under capitalism. Do you see what that tells us? Russia and communism are not the final enemy; powerful domination in every system wants to maintain its privilege. Now as we hear talk of the destruction of the Berlin Wall, we find that half the people in West Berlin in fact do not want it torn down! I'll bet I can tell you which half: Those who have put their identity and security in the economic system. So also, maleness is not the problem, but male pretensions of power and winning. These towers of Babel have cost men their own souls for too long — along with the bodies, spirits, and dignity of much of the rest of the world.

Pyramids are always pyramids of sacrifice. Whether it is the hundreds of thousands of slaves creating monuments to Egyptian kings, the sacrificial victims offering their hearts to Aztec gods, or the underpaid maids and janitors in the tourist hotels of the world, someone always has to give his life or her life so that someone else can be "special." When that specialness is idealized and protected instead of avoided and made unnecessary, as Jesus taught, we have the destructive and dark side of power. Jesus struck at the nerve center of such power when he empowered honest human relationships instead of degrees of religious worthiness. Jesus built circles instead of pyramids. What they could not forgive him for, even on the cross, was that he announced the necessary destruction of the holy temple. "Not a stone will stand on a stone. Everything will be destroyed" (Mark 13:2). He knew that the temple, now divided into courts of worthiness, was not a place where God was first as much as a place that kept the central storehouse economy in control and the widow with her "mite" outside. Thus he revealingly called it "the treasury" (Mark 12:41) and committed the unforgivable sin of overturning the tables of "those who were selling and buying there" (Luke 19:45). In attacking the temple, he attacked Judaism's final tower and democratized religion once and for all. But like Aaron the first priest, we priests have been building golden calves and golden temples ever since. With priests and ministers, the assumption is that if it is good for religion, it is good for God. "False!" said Jesus.

Even the tower of Babel incident referred to at the beginning of this chapter reveals that God had to scatter and confuse the one language of the men who had built the pretentious tower "to make a name for ourselves" (Gen. 11:4). Here we have the anomaly of a God who separates and divides people when they have structured themselves wrongly. In an early style of perestroika, God reverses this process at Pentecost when tongues of fire now unite the different languages into one universal language of the Spirit: "each hearing in their own language about the wonderful works of God" (Acts 2:11). Circles of communication, networks of nations, true brotherhood and sisterhood are finally possible in this new people who are born of God's Spirit. And it is no accident that God the Spirit is presented in a feminine and maternal image from which we are "born" (John 3:5–8). Immediately after the giving of the Pentecost Spirit we have the further birth of real and honest community: "The faithful all lived together and owned everything in common; they sold their goods and possessions and shared out of the proceeds according to each one's need" (Acts 2:44–45). We can only imagine fondly since it has rarely happened again. Francis of Assisi tried. The vow of poverty was an attempt. But the patriarchal need for domination and possession preferred towers and basilicas to human community, degrees of worthiness instead of honest human relationships. Dare I list the line-up? Pope, curia, cardinals, metropolitans, archbishops, bishops, vicar generals, monsignors, priests, deacons, subdeacons (recently rejected as unnecessary!), exorcists, acolytes, lectors, and porters constitute the *cleros,* or "separated ones." If there is any worthiness left, it is graciously dispensed to the *laos,* the 99 percent of the membership who are told exactly how they can be worthy. Forgive my sarcasm, but it is intentional and long overdue. God's reputation is at stake.

The feminine insight is a rediscovery of Jesus' spirit, a re-emergence of a well-suppressed truth, an eventual political upheaval, a certain reform of our hearing of the Gospel and someday perhaps the very structures of the churches — and all proceeding from a "knowing" in the mother's womb — exactly where we received Christ from the first time.

It was no accident that we Catholics had a psychological need to exalt Mary to the role of a Goddess. I am not sure if it was an inherent need to balance ourselves, a disguise for the patriarchy underneath, a love affair with the denied woman within, or just a work of the Spirit, but it is an overwhelming example of instinct winning out over logic and theology. So much so, in fact, that the only two infallible statements of this Roman patriarchal Church are ironically the Assumption of the physical body of Mary into heaven and her privileged choice and protection by God called the "Immaculate Conception." Furthermore, we even celebrate her "Coronation as Queen of heaven and earth." I'm really all for it, but none of these are found in Scripture or public revelation. Amazing how this male Church was always feminist — and unwittingly ready to bend all the rules to say so! That healthy instinct has now come to our service and we call it "women stuff." Sorry, boys, we Catholics have always been there. Proud and orthodox in public, but Mama's boys whenever we could find an excuse for it. It's not new or liberal or dangerous; it's very old, quite conservative, and as traditional as Mary and the Eight Beatitudes.

The feminist insight explains the vast majority of Jesus' teachings, a male acting very differently in an almost totally patriarchal Jewish society. Like Mary, the Church also has "treasured these things in her heart" (Luke 2:19). Only in time are they ready to come forth, like Jesus from her womb. Jesus would never have broken through as the fresh Word of the Father if he had, for example, acted non-violently in a feminine body. It would not have been Divine Revelation because we expect and demand that *women* be patient, nurturing, forgiving, healing, self-effacing, and self-sacrificing. Women are expected to be non-violent in a violent male society (look at our one-sided attitude toward rape, adultery, physical abuse, and, in many cultures, divorce), but we are still not prepared for males or institutions or nations to act non-violently. That is why God *had* to become incarnate for us in the body of a man. Unfortunately, we kept the name and image of Jesus to exalt male leadership, but basically rejected most of Jesus' teachings as impractical and unreasonable in the pyramidal "real world" of Church and state. As indeed they are! We conveniently fit Jesus back into our more practical way of being a religious institution — and lost most of his unique and revolutionary strategy for dealing with human evil. Now we find ourselves helpless and without the tools to deal with war, greed, and the endless whimsy of the individual ego.

No one was wicked or intentional in all of this, nor is it all wrong and lost, but it does show the depth and disguise of evil. Power is surely not intrinsically wrong, but it is very dangerous and, in my opinion, only spiritually mature people can handle it. Power, another word for the Spirit in Scripture, is most effective when it is clearly recognized as such and clearly shared as a common but diverse gift. At Pentecost the Spirit came down on "all" (Acts 2:1), giving them the power to recognize and affirm life within themselves and in one another. That is the richest meaning of authority. It is the power to author life in others. That power is not exclusively or even primarily held by men. It seems to me that should be self-evident. At the present moment of history unbalanced male consciousness has given us both totalitarian communism and greedy capitalism, neither of them seeking the common good of humanity. They are both pyramids of sacrifice and both afraid of circles of truth and justice.

I see nothing in the New Testament that tells me Jesus intended or desired his new community to be modeled on the power structures of the Roman Empire. I further see nothing in the life narrative of Peter the fisherman that tells me that he can be expected to do anything but doubt, bungle, deny, and run. But he also professes love and stands as a full prophetic image of the de facto life of the hierarchy and the Church. Jesus' love of Peter tells me that he is willing to work with just such human brokenness — just as he is willing to work with all the rest of the world that is unsuitable, out of order, unorthodox, and even sinful. That, unfortunately, is what patriarchy is unwilling and unable to do. It demands an infallible pope and a "worthy" people. The love of power does not have the capacity to nurture anything that it cannot explain or control. The exclusive rule of the fathers not only makes community and justice impossible but also holds Christ's salvation at the level of salvation theories and techniques that educated clerics can be "right" about. The starving millions deserve a better God than that. They deserve the Father that Jesus knew.

The Father that Jesus knew looks amazingly like what most cultures would call "Mother." In Luke 15, the story of the prodigal son, Jesus makes his most complete presentation of the character of this Father, whom he called God. The father is in every way the total opposite of the male patriarch and even rejects his older son's appeal to a world of worthiness and merit. He not only allows the younger son to make choices against him, but even empowers him to do so by giving him the money! After his bad mistakes, the father still refuses his right to restore order or impose a penance even though the prodigal son offers to serve as a hired servant. Both his leaving and his returning are treated as necessary but painful acts of adult freedom. In every way he can, the father makes mutuality and vulnerability possible. As Sr. Sandra Schneiders says, this new kind of father "refuses to own us, demand our submission, or punish our rebellion. Father God is one who respects our freedom, mourns our alienation, waits patiently for our return, and accepts our love as pure gift. . . . God tries to educate the older brother, and through him all disciples who prefer the security of law to the adventure of grace." In an absolutely reeling conclusion, she says, "The power God refuses to assume over us is surely not given by God to any human being." Not even to the Church that must always live in the image of the heavenly Father.

All this "woman stuff" is not only important, it is the other half of conversion, the other half of salvation, the other half of wholeness that completes God's work of art. I believe this mystery is imaged in the Woman of the twelfth chapter of the Apocalypse: "pregnant, and in labor, crying aloud in the pangs of childbirth . . . and finally escaping into the desert until her time."

Could this be the time? I think it must be. The world is tired of Pentagons and pyramids, empires and corporations that only abort God's child. The East has stopped playing the other half of our game and now speaks disturbingly of glasnost and perestroika. The West is alive with liberation movements at every level of consciousness, with race, gender, and economic issues (prestige, power, and possessions!) at the forefront. Even the Church is finding the humility to recognize its fear of the subjective and the personal and its unlawful marriage to the systems of power and control. The woman is coming out of her desert escape, with no possibility of return. Too many of us have seen her gift. The Holy Child Wisdom is among us and the vision is compelling. We *can* live and think differently.

Yes, this woman stuff is very important. More than this white male priest ever imagined or desired! My God was too small and too male. Now I don't know how to fight with a woman. What I, what we, need to learn is to make love to Her, to recognize and affirm Her gifts, to understand that She is intrinsic to divine and human wholeness.

QUESTIONS and ANSWERS

Q. *At the conclusion you said that you don't know how to fight with a woman. I didn't understand that at all.*

A. I start from the assumption that authentic faith has something to do with fighting God, and I'm not sure I know how best to engage with a God who is also feminine. I know the rules of the game for struggling with a man, but I have less understanding of how you struggle with a woman. That's also surely connected to the fact that I'm not married.

Q. *What's your response to theologian Christa Mulack's image of God? She thinks the goddess is missing in Christianity.*

A. I believe in the Trinity. But still I agree with Christa Mulack that we have to find the maternal face of God. I believe it's very simple to look on the Spirit/Spiritess as feminine. We can also say that the power of the relationship that occurs between the Father and the Son is something feminine. I believe that in the Christian tradition there have always been people who by means of prayer have pressed through to find the female face of God. This is certainly one of the possibilities for correctly integrating into our faith the medieval veneration of Mary, or even later forms of piety like the veneration of the Sacred Heart. Somehow we have always sensed that our image of God is too masculine. That's why we've tried in different ways to venerate this female face of God as well. In Genesis it says point blank: We are made in the image of God, masculine and feminine. From this verse alone it should be obvious that God is not a man, but that men and women reflect the image of God. I don't believe, however, that this means we have to give up the doctrine of the Trinity.

Q. *Richard Rohr, the caller to the men in the wilderness, do you really believe that the two hundred most powerful families in the U.S.A. who control everything are aiming at gentleness and weakness? Do you really believe that the three million people who are wandering around homeless in America have been found by the powerful? Do you really believe that God is so strong in America that weakness is winning, and not strength?*

A. You've focused on the right question. I believe this is one of the reasons why Jesus so often asked sadly, "When the Son of man comes, will he find faith on earth?" It was obvious to Jesus that he would always represent a minority position. He saw clearly that his community would always remain a little flock. And nevertheless one has to say that all over the world you can sense a growing awareness of the dignity of the individual. There is a growing distrust of power, dictatorships, and mechanisms of oppression. But you're right: Our country is built on a mythology of power, and it'll be very hard to deprive the system of its power. America has to acknowledge its shadow. I believe the Vietnam War was the encounter with our shadow, but we forgot about it too quickly.

Q. *Can you as a Catholic say something about Mary?*

A. I believe it's important that we let Mary be a *person.* As Catholics we have drifted too far in the opposite direction. The image that Mary *is one of us* helps us to identify with her and to duplicate her attitude. That way she'll much more readily become a graphic image for the Church and for salvation. You can put someone on a pedestal and thereby prevent any authentic relation with that person. When we do this with women it's called in psychology the "Madonna complex." We put Mary on such a lofty pedestal that she has no real meaning and no real message for us. In Latin America they have no difficulty discovering in the Magnificat that Mary is a woman who fights with them for liberation down at the grassroots level. She does this, of course, in her quality as a poor woman from Nazareth — and not as the larger-than-life Mother of God. That's why I suggest we love Mary as a *woman* who was chosen by God.

8   The Social and Political Vocation of Christians (Mark 10)

PAUL TELLS US that the word of God is a perfect mirror of freedom. I believe the first task of God's word
is to confront us with ourselves, with our truth. And this
confrontation will lead, we hope, to changing our lives,
to building our lives on the great truth that Jesus calls
the "Reign of God." It seems to me that only after we've
changed our lives does the Gospel promise comfort. In my
opinion the great danger facing a prosperous Christianity
is that we have exactly reversed this process. We let ourselves be comforted first, before letting the perfect mirror
of freedom confront us with ourselves. And that's why our
religion remains so schizophrenic.

Among Christians there are pray-ers and activists. The
activists don't understand anything about prayer, and the
prayers of the pious seldom lead to involvement. The whole
Gospel suffers from that, because neither of the two has the
whole Christ or real credibility. Our Bible texts today will
explain how different the call these people receive must be.
In the tenth chapter of Mark two different "callings" follow
in rapid succession, first the calling of the rich young man

A talk given in the Old Library, Giessen, March 19, 1990.

and then of the blind man Bartimaeus. First the section on Jesus and the rich young man (Mark 10:17–27).

"As he was setting out on his journey, a man ran up and knelt before him, and asked him, 'Good Teacher, what must I do to inherit eternal life?'" Observe that the rich young man is very polite, very respectful toward Jesus. But we notice right away that Jesus doesn't take the bait of this flattery. He knows the danger of a language that's too nice, that really wants to keep the other at arm's length. (We've found that the word "nice" does not occur once in the New Testament. But bourgeois Christianity continually revolves around being "nice.") "And Jesus said to him: 'Why do you call me good? No one is good but God alone.'" Jesus immediately points beyond himself. Isn't that interesting? If *we* said that Jesus wasn't good, we'd be treated as heretics. Jesus wanted people to come to grips with reality, not with ideals and images. Images and ideals allow us to remain in love with ourselves, but Jesus preferred us to be in love with truth.

That's why his answer comes out sounding brusque and not very understanding. He simply lists the Ten Commandments: "Do not kill, Do not commit adultery, Do not steal, Do not bear false witness," in the proper order of the Commandments as we know them. But before he mentions the Fourth Commandment he makes a little insertion. Before he says, "Honor your father and mother," he says, "Do not defraud." Where does that come from? It's not one of the Ten Commandments; it's evidently what he's reproaching the young man for. The young man belongs to the large landowners and naturally wants to defend himself right away. He wants to prove that despite his wealth he is, religiously speaking, justified: "Teacher, all these I have observed from my youth." He has completely missed the point of Jesus' adding the line, "Do not defraud."

Jesus straightway looks at him and loves him. He knows that justice isn't possible until we've experienced love. He knows that this man's sin is at bottom not a personal thing, but a kind of objective dilemma that he's trapped in. That's why he tries to tell him how he can get out of the lie he's caught in, how he can again ground his life on the truth instead of on lies.

"Jesus said, 'You lack one thing; go, sell what you have, and give to the poor.'" That's what you have to do, otherwise you won't be free. Because your money builds on a lie, and you have to base your life on the truth. "And you will have treasure in heaven." Only when you face this challenge, can you "come, follow me." The rich young man isn't personally bad; he's simply part of the system in which he's stuck. And Jesus calls him to distance himself from it. This is the only example in the Gospel of Mark of a person whom Jesus calls and becomes a non-follower, a non-disciple. "At that saying his countenance fell, and he went away sorrowful, for he had great possessions." We notice that every time Jesus challenges those who have power and wealth he never calls them personally evil or malevolent. Instead he points to the fact that they're blind, that they can't see. He tells them that they have to leave this system, because otherwise they'll never learn to see.

For far too long we've preached the Gospel only in a individualistic fashion. We thought we could have a personal relationship with Jesus without calling into question the systems and institutions we participate in and to which we belong. In the first few years when I worked with young people in Cincinnati, I preached the Gospel and the young people fell in love with Christ. They believed that they were converted, that they were "saved." But then they went back into the American system, and it turned out that the conversion didn't go very deep. Genuine evangelization must be good news for the individual and *at the same time* for society, for the nation, for the institution. I think the great blind spot of European and American Christianity consists in the fact that we can't see that the Gospel isn't aimed just at the individual, but also at society.

Thus women, the poor, and the base communities are raising altogether different questions, and altogether different answers will come to light. We can no longer so easily thrust aside, as we used to, the unequivocal message of the sort of passage we have just now read.

Perhaps the poor see themselves in the second part of chapter 10 of Mark's Gospel, namely with the calling of the poor blind man, Bartimaeus. We see a paradox here: Bartimaeus is the blind man who isn't blind — in contrast to the rich man, who's really poor. Between these two stories Mark presents a great warning from Jesus against the real enemies of the Reign of God. These are the three great obsessions: power, prestige, and possessions. In the Sermon on the Mount it's quite clear that these are the three great barriers we have to overcome to understand Jesus and understand the Reign of God. But in Christianity we have always been concerned with ecclesiological questions, with sacramental questions, sacerdotal questions, and, needless to say, sexual questions — questions that Jesus practically never bothered with.

It seems to me as if a kind of shadow screen had been slipped between us and Jesus here. We slide it in between so that we don't have to see the real questions. This is called a diversionary tactic. We probably choose it unconsciously and in all innocence because our ego finds enormously tricky ways to avoid self-surrender. Our ego finds incredibly imaginative ways to avoid letting go — even when we claim that we believe in the absolute authority of the Bible. Let's all be honest and admit that our various denominations have one and all been only selectively obedient and have picked out only certain Bible verses that backed up our theological biases.

But every time Jesus deals with the real subjects of this world, namely with power and control, and with economic questions that would demand real change from us (not just changes in the head, but in our whole life) all the churches — without exception — have shoved those teachings aside and ignored them. None of us is ready for the great Christ, for the whole Christ; none of us is ready for the story that Christ offers us — except for poor blind people like Bartimaeus.

> And they came to Jericho; and as he was leaving Jericho with his disciples and a great multitude, Bartimaeus, a blind beggar, the son of Timaeus, was sitting by the roadside. And when he heard that it was Jesus of Nazareth, he began to cry out and say, "Jesus, Son of David, have mercy on me!" And many rebuked him, telling him to be silent; but he cried out all the more, "Jesus, Son of David, have mercy one me!"

This poor man isn't polite like the rich man. He shouts, he interrupts what's going on; and we see immediately how the disciples get irritated because he's not abiding by the appropriate rules of etiquette. And we see how his words differ from the words of the rich young man: The rich young man asks: "How can *I* get eternal life?" He's always concerned with himself; it *is* a kind of enlightened egoism, but it's still egoism. And a large part of Christianity has so far refused to admit how egotistical it actually is. We've claimed we love Christ, but in reality this has been just a protective façade for hiding our understandable self-interest. In Bartimaeus we see someone who's not asking anything at all for himself; he simply cries out twice for mercy. He knows that he's empty. He knows that he has nothing of what perhaps he should or must have.

This time it's Jesus who goes to him — the opposite of what happened in the first story. "And Jesus stopped and said, 'Call him.' And they called the blind man, saying to him, 'Take heart; rise; he is calling you.' " Even the disciples are surprised that Jesus is obviously interested in this completely useless person. The gestures of this blind man are the exact reverse of the rich young man's gestures: "And throwing off his mantle, he sprang up and came to Jesus." Here we see a man who's not covering himself, but giving himself away. He springs up full of naiveté, full of foolishness, full of youthful enthusiasm; and Jesus asks him: "What do you want me to do for you?"

This time Jesus takes the initiative: He knows that he can really give this man something — the rich young man wasn't open to that. With this man there's an openness, a readiness, an emptiness. He is not stuffed full of prefabricated answers and theology; he's full of desire, full of longing. "And the blind man said, 'Master, let me receive my sight.' "

We have on the one hand the rich man, who thinks he can see but who in reality can see nothing and, as a counterimage, the blind man, who can't see and yet in reality does see. "And Jesus said to him, 'Go your way; your faith has made you well.' " He doesn't say, your orthodoxy, your correct doctrine has made you well; he doesn't say, your obedience to the Commandments has made you well. The rich young man is anxious to prove to Jesus that he has kept all the Commandments. We have no proof that this blind man ever did anything "right" in his life, but Jesus says: "'Go your way; your faith has made you well.' And immediately he received his sight and followed him on *the way*." And we know what this way means if we read the next verse, because the first verse of chapter 11 says: "They drew near to Jerusalem." This is no gentle Gospel, we're evidently talking about the way of the cross, about a way of imitation and discipleship that calls upon us to surrender and let go.

But we must honestly confess that the Gospel has in many ways been lured into a trap by our society and culture. The Gospel is for the most part held by cultures of affluence. This is a society where we not only need more and more things, but where we keep demanding more and where we think we have a right to keep getting more. Our whole feeling of self-worth depends on our getting more, on our doing more, on our always climbing higher and higher. And that's why the story of the rich young man is aimed at us.

If we go through the Gospels and read them, we notice that with Jesus things always go back and forth: One time he preaches the Gospel to the oppressors and another time to the oppressed. Unfortunately it's the victors who almost every time reject and refuse him. And it's the victims of this world who almost always understand him. It almost looks as if we had to go below and off to the margin to become at all capable of hearing the Gospel. On the margin the social and political implications of the Gospel become quite obvious and clear. There we learn that we can't use Jesus to defend and maintain our position of power and wealth or to keep up for our own sake a positive self-image as polite and decent people.

It could be that Jesus will lead us to a place where we ourselves don't even know any more whether we're holy, where all we know is that we have to do what we have to do, where we have to obey the word that we've heard in our heart. Often we don't even get the satisfaction of being in the right; and there's no security that everyone will agree with us. Perhaps that's why Jesus says, "I chose you out of the world, and therefore the world hates you" (John 15:19). Because this Gospel doesn't bless the existing system; it leads us to the edges where freedom might be found. It does so in such a way that we can return to the world, without being addictively dependent on it any more, so that we can return to the suffering and joys of this world, without letting ourselves be seduced by its false promises on either side.

I think a large part of Jesus' teaching is a critique of "mammon sickness." Jesus describes that disease as follows: Those afflicted by it are continually driven by unrest, cares, and anxiety, because the present isn't enough for them. But for those grounded in Christ the present contains great abundance, even though we don't yet live in the full Reign of God. This is precisely the peace that the world can't give, and the peace the world can't take away from us. It's the only real gift we can bring into the existing system: the health (*salus*) of a central life.

No political system, no explanation of the world can be anything else than a mixture of the Reign of God and what isn't the Reign of God. Of course, it's our responsibility to carry as much as possible of the Reign of God into this world, but no social or political system will ever be identical with the Reign of God. Yet if we live in the fullness

of the Here and Now — and this is the gift of the crucified and simultaneously risen Christ — then we no longer
run anxiously around to get a definitive explanation of the
world; we can live with *what is*.

Seven years ago I was with Jim Wallis in Germany. We
had worked a great deal with the peace movement at the
time, and we had preached in many parts of the country
as we had in the U.S. We took part in protests, we prayed,
and we studied the issues of war and peace. After we had
done all that, suddenly this fellow Gorbachev appeared,
and the old rigid fronts started to move. Even if it seemed
that the "New Jerusalem" was on the point of descending
from heaven, we couldn't claim that our work had produced the arrival of the "New Jerusalem." Nevertheless,
we had to do what we did. Because why should God give
us something that we don't even want? Why should God
give us something that we're not ready to work and do our
utmost for? Why should God give us something that we
at most pray for, but don't strive for? God doesn't believe
just in our prayers. That's why we do our work, launch
protests, and at the same time wait every moment for the
"New Jerusalem" to descend from the heavens. I believe
this is the great mystery of co-creation to which God has
invited us. Mammon disease makes us completely deaf and
blind to this full reality.

About ten years ago I was invited to dinner by a family
in Cincinnati (it's always nice to invite the pastor). This nice
Italian family had three charming children. The youngest
was named Christopher; he had big brown eyes, and he
had just learned to run. After dinner he ran through the
living room and fell down the stairs. But we didn't hear
a sound or any crying, so we were very worried because
we didn't know whether he had injured himself. So we ran

to the stairway, and there Christopher lay at the foot of the stairs. And his big brown eyes looked up inquiringly at his father, as if to say, "Did I hurt myself?" His father ran down to him, took him in his arms, and the instant his father's arms enfolded him, the boy began to scream and cry. I wondered why this little boy needed seven seconds before he felt pain, but at the same moment the answer occurred to me (and I knew at once that this would be a terrific example for a sermon): The little boy couldn't feel and admit the pain until he was sufficiently sure that love was there.

It seems to me that a Christian is a person who has the freedom to feel the pain that's part of being human. This means a person who has the freedom to enter into solidarity with the suffering of the world, precisely because this person is sure of the Father's love. Without that love we're deaf and our feelings go numb. And we can't spend our whole lives desperately trying to experience this love again; we have to leave the first step behind and move ahead to further steps.

The problem with so many churches in our country is that every worship service tries to produce step one of Christian existence. And that's why we don't get any mature, grown-up Christians, but often very childish Christians who are busy with their own feelings and nothing else. The final effect of mammon disease is that we've lived with a split consciousness, that we're incapable of really integrating faith with the tragic mystery of things. For people in the world of business, the world of finance, the world of commerce, or the world of insurance, faith is neither enlightening nor comfortable. If money doesn't quite explicitly and in all its consequences come under God's Reign, it won't remain a neutral force very long; it will seize dominion for itself. When we speak of God's sovereignty, we too often mean a nominal and honorary sovereignty, not a real one that has consequences, that changes our lifestyle in this world.

In America we say, "Money talks." I'm afraid money is the *only* thing doing the talking! Although we claim that Jesus is the Lord, it's obvious that in reality power, prestige, and possessions are the lords. Of course this holds us back from the freedom of the true children of God. I don't believe that there's a concrete goal we have to shoot for at all costs; rather Jesus gives us a process, he demands of us a way of life that he calls *forgiveness*, a way of life that does not hold on but lets go. It is a new way of seeing, so that human community is possible. I don't presume to be so clever as to know what the ideal community should look like. My task is to live the Reign of God here and now — not just privately for myself, but in an interconnected way, that is, a way that influences my economy, my finances, and my political position, that influences how I use the goods of this earth. This is the way of Bartimaeus. It's the way of the blind man who in reality isn't blind at all. I believe that the Gospel invites us all to enter upon this way.

QUESTIONS and ANSWERS

Q. *How can I alleviate the world's pain unless I have mammon?*

A. I said we have to find the place of real freedom from which we can return into the world. I didn't say that Jesus was against possessions on principle; I said he was against idol worship. As soon as we *really* abjure this world's money, we have the freedom to go back and use that money and do some good with it. But we have to keep on critically testing ourselves so that we don't deceive ourselves. It's easy enough to repeat the saying, "I'm in the world, but not of it."

We have to discover very concretely and specifically how badly, for example, we identify with money. Only when our money is taken away do we learn how much we're possessed by our possessions. Don't think this can take place in your head. The father of my order, Francis of Assisi, was fully convinced that poverty has to take on concrete dimensions. This is an altogether practical matter, when we see how many billion people live on this little planet. We have to find real and realistic ways to be brothers and sisters to these people. The goods of this world have to be used, of course, but in a way that's honest and in which sharing plays a much larger role.

Q. *You've spoken about not making a value system out of money. But we're a part of the system. Can you give practical examples of how we can escape the system?*

A. First, it's a question of lifestyle. In America there was a woman named Dorothy Day, the founder of the Catholic Worker movement; and because of her all over America today there are houses for the homeless and people in need of shelter. This woman lived a poverty-stricken life. She said, "I'd like to live my life so close to the bottom that when the system collapses I don't have far to fall."

Of course, the more we're tied up in the system, the fewer questions we can ask. I wonder, for example, why did Jesus say we shouldn't take oaths? One interpretation is that every oath is a promise we make to a system;

we must call into question the "oaths" we've made to institutions and armies. Our only commitment must be to
the Body of Christ and to humanity. No individual can
carry the cross alone. Only when groups of radical young
people get together can they create a kind of counter-
system that sees to it that they're less dependent on the
old system. I think this is one of the reasons many of us
have spent time building communities. It was a sad experience for me to note that most of these communities
have disintegrated. Still we can't deny that covenant communities were a wonderful *school* for thousands of people.
They created a network of "ties that bind," a network of
community-minded people, of men and women who know
how to connect with others, who know how to share,
who know how to let go. I say this so that you yourselves may contribute to creating such networks. Without
them there's no practicable method for standing outside the
status quo.

Q. *How can political structures be changed? Do we have to
reject all political structures?*

A. I wouldn't want you to take what I've said as anti-
structural. I'm simply objecting to the idolization of any
given structure as the perfect one. The patriarchal image of
God has seduced us into building up and idealizing pyramidal structures. If I understand Jesus correctly, he seems
to talk more about circles than about pyramids. His first description of the Church is "two or three who are gathered
in my name." But when unredeemed men place themselves at the top, they create pyramids. And pyramids are
always built on the sacrifices of others. To build the Egyptian pyramids hundreds of thousands of slaves had to give

their lives; the Mayan temples were built so that human sacrifices could be offered on top of them.

When more feminine insights gain greater influence, better structures too will slowly develop; they'll be shaped less like pyramids and more like circles. And that's exactly what I'm concerned about: How to create a world where it's possible to live as brothers and sisters, instead of us pastors quarreling over what the true priest should look like, about who has the true theology, who gets to heaven and who doesn't. These are the chimeras of academically educated males. We need circles where we can be vulnerable and honest, where the prevailing atmosphere is one of healing and sharing of wisdom.

Q. *How is the world to function without the rich at the top?*

A. I don't know, but I also don't believe that this is really your problem, that it's anything you have to resolve. Not that you shouldn't deal with economic issues. The contemplative attitude takes the liberty of not knowing about such things. Haven't we as Christians always had the feeling that we had to have the answer to everything? Why have we made faith into a kind of security blanket? We've taken what for Jesus was a journey into the unknown and turned in into a life insurance policy. I'd be glad to find a clear economic plan in the Gospel; but the only thing Jesus gave us unequivocal enlightenment about was the great danger of wealth. He said quite clearly that we're not supposed to get rich. We live differently in the poverty and ignorance of faith — which consists in our having no plan. Faith has a much higher price than I ever would have expected; the willingness to walk in darkness makes other people see you as naive.

Q. *What do you think about the charismatic movements? Do you see there the danger of an enlightened egoism?*

A. My community, "New Jerusalem," was for a time one of the most exciting and lively charismatic communities in the country. And around the beginning of the 1970s I had the reputation of being the great charismatic pastor of young people. But ultimately I too realized that the charismatic movement had its shadow side. First, it's much too depen-dent on feelings. You don't mature in the faith if you need too many emotional experiences — that's quite obvious. In my opinion the charismatic movement has an exaggerated resurrection theology and a fear of the cross. That's why you find there only half the paschal mystery. (In *Discov-ering the Enneagram* I call this the energy of the SEVEN, but that's only one of the possible ways of describing the matter.)

On the other hand, the charismatic movement is a wonderful point of departure. Some of the most effec-tive social activists in our country spent two or three years during the 1970s in prayer groups. They them-selves admit that the charismatic experience taught them the immediacy and the warmth of the love of God. They learned there to thirst after holiness. But these same people also say that after two or three years they stopped growing, that nothing new unfolded. It's a won-derful, maybe even *necessary*, first step of faith, and I mean that quite seriously, but the next steps simply don't happen there. We must be led beyond the world of feelings into the world of real faith, where we don't con-tinually have to reactivate first emotions. Mature faith knows its ground and yet is also able to include and integrate.

The best point of departure is conservative, because first you need a clear feeling for your own boundaries. First, you have to learn: What does it mean to be in Christ, or not to be in Christ? You see this psychologically in every person who grows in his or her faith: The more you become sure of your own center, the more you can also open your boundaries. Otherwise you'll spend your whole life defending those boundaries. This is like a litmus test for recognizing immature Christianity. Nevertheless we have to be patient and allow ourselves to take certain steps toward growth. A mature Christian is capable of going beyond all previous boundaries and suddenly discovering Christ where he or she would never have suspected.

I think this is the clear meaning of the story in chapter 25 of Matthew: The people were suddenly able to discover Christ in the least of their brothers and sisters, and not just in other charismatics, not just with other evangelicals. Otherwise, all you have is a collective self-love. Then the group is, so to speak, just an extension of my own ego. "You have to use the same Christian jargon as I do, so that we can be together." But this isn't the freedom of the children of God. Such people will never unite or reconcile anything, because their life at bottom keeps getting smaller and smaller. Real Christians are able to discover and love Christ in the not-me, in the totally other — but this always means taking a step beyond previous boundaries. I don't believe that the charismatic movement has really given its members the capacity to do that. In any case not in our country. Nevertheless I repeat: It helps a great deal in the first stage of faith. Our overintellectual interpretation of the Gospel has needed the charismatic movement to get out its cerebral box.

Q. *I didn't understand what you meant by saying, I have to change myself before I can be comforted. Where am I to change?*

A. That's exactly why I chose the story of the rich young man. The change has to be very concrete, very immediate, and very practical, otherwise it's just an intellectual thing. Jesus asks the rich young man to move from here to there — and he meant economically. For most of us this means turning to people who are different from us. This is the only thing that can liberate us from our egocentric attitude. Maybe it means that as younger men and women we go to our elders, or maybe as healthy persons we go to the physically and mentally handicapped, or if we're homophobic we work in an AIDS hospital. But we all have to set out into a world in which we're not number 1, where the others whom we meet are not just an expanded version of ourselves.

I believe that circumstances change us, not sermons. We're changed when we move on to a new place and when we expose ourselves to the truth of a different standpoint, one that's not our own. What else is *metanoia*, or conversion, supposed to mean in the New Testament? It means to go to a different place; and this practical step will see to it that our growth as Christians is something real, something earthbound. Otherwise there is always the danger that our so-called love of Christ will be just a disguised love of self.

You see, religion is a very dangerous business. I always say, it's the surest way to avoid God. The scribes and the Pharisees in the Bible illustrate this well enough. If spiritual conversion doesn't lead us to letting go of and surrendering our lives and being able to go beyond ourselves, I believe it remains just an illusion; not real love of God but love of self. I know that from my own experience, because it often happened that way with me.

Q. *Should we Christians opt for socialism or for capitalism?*

A. Both systems strike me as showing the incapacity of Christians to integrate what belongs together. We've kept on making the Gospel into an ideology that you can agree with or not, instead of a process of reconciliation, in which nobody is right and we all stand humbly before God. I think that our imperialistic view of Christianity has contributed to this, as well as our inability to take seriously much of the Bible, e.g., Jesus' extensive teachings on riches. It's very easy for us in the capitalistic West to lean back and say: "Look, everything they were doing over there was wrong." But socialism basically grew out of the failure, and followed the pattern, of Western Christianity.

I believe that's why we have to find a third way in between these two systems: I mean the truth of a society built on solidarity, which socialism doubtless bears within itself. When I took the vow of poverty and promised to share all material goods with other Franciscans, why did people say, "How holy and wonderful that is!" while when other people do it, it's suddenly called an evil system? Of course, the difference was that we did it voluntarily, and the others were forced to do it. The gift of our capitalist system is our commitment to freedom. As you surely all know, the definition of this freedom is generally very hollow and self-centered. It has little to do with the freedom of the children of God.

Many have discovered under communism that less is more. We in the West no longer believe that. We've turned the Gospel into a kind of spiritual capitalism: We want to *get* grace, *we* want to be "saved," we want to *have* security — the private ego wants to go on accumulating more and more. And spiritual possessions are the most dangerous of all.

So, to answer your question: There is, on the one hand, the truth of community and, on the other hand, the truth of individual freedom. The Church is the only laboratory that can bring these two truths under one roof. I hope you're the sort of Church that can learn something from what we experienced in Dresden and Leipzig. And I'm sure that communism has much to learn from the West. Every part of the body of Christ in the whole world has a special gift. You shouldn't doubt yours. But this also means that we have to distinguish quite clearly between what's light and what's darkness, what is genuine freedom and what is false freedom. And this is certainly the responsibility of the West Germans and of Americans.

Q. *What makes a person a Christian? What characterizes a Christian in contrast to the non-Christian?*

A. A Christian is someone who's animated by the spirit of Christ, a person in whom the spirit of Christ can work. That doesn't always mean that you consciously know what you are doing. As it says in Matthew 25: "When have we seen you hungry? When have we seen you thirsty?" These people had no idea that they did what they did for Christ, and that it was Christian. But Christ said: "Because you did it, you did it for me." This is the final consequence of the Incarnation of God. The Word is no longer word; it has really become flesh. That means it never depends upon whether we say the right words, but whether we live the right reality. A Christian is someone who's inhabited by the spirit of Christ, which is a gift, as we know, yet a gift that we can say yes to without fully understanding the gift!

Q. *You said before that in a certain sense Latin America is converting the American Church and that you hope the same thing for Europe. I find that a very hopeful statement. Could you explain more precisely how this is happening in America, and how it might come over to us?*

A. I hope I didn't sound too optimistic. It's not as if the American Church is really converted. Still it's amazing how many people are slowly realizing what's at stake here. Last month I was in a Protestant seminary in Dallas. A professor there told me that he himself had noticed how denominational differences are becoming less and less important. There are Christian men and women who are moving toward the perspective of justice, and there are others who aren't. That's the most meaningful division. You can be in a college class or in a seminar and only discover after many days, "Oh, you're Catholic. Oh, you're Protestant." The more the focus is on the questions addressed in the Sermon on the Mount, the more irrelevant the historical confessional differences and their formulations are getting. That doesn't mean it was all false, but they have less meaning and concrete significance. The "preferential option for the poor" is now a broadly re-discovered Gospel ideal. It came from the Latin American Church.

Q. *I'd like to get into the question of the new communities and the simple life one more time. Don't these new forms of life also present the danger of being just new kinds of indulgences? You know, following the motto: "The less I have, the better I am.*

The longer I live in the community, the better I am." Do you see this danger too?

A. Sure. That's the danger of spiritual riches. The corruption of the best is the worst of all. Our gift and our sin are two sides of the same coin. Andreas Ebert and I try to present that idea in our book *Discovering the Enneagram*. We can do the right thing for the wrong reasons. But that doesn't mean we shouldn't try to do the right thing. The point is that we always have to keep its dark side in mind too. It's always very humbling when you do that. Everything that becomes an end in itself — except for God — becomes an idol, including Christian community. Maybe that's even one of the reasons why so many communities have fallen apart. We were forced again to press on to a deeper level and to ask: What is faith now?

I compare everything that belongs to the Church with fingers that point to the moon. We're all just means to the end, not the end itself. As soon as we begin to argue about the fingers or to protect the fingers or to quarrel over who has the best fingers, instead of noticing that all these fingers point to the moon, then we're disobeying the First Commandment, which forbids us to create idols. Christian community can become an idol too; even the Bible can become an idol. The pope can be an idol. The sacraments can be idols. And the more spiritual it looks, the more dangerous it is. The spiritual life is a very risky adventure, but what's the alternative?

9 Less Is More — Paths to a Spirituality of the Simple Life (Luke 19)

F OR THE PAST FOUR YEARS I've been living in the American Southwest, in New Mexico. It's one of the poorer states in America, though also one of the most beautiful. It's a very militarized state, where the atomic bomb was discovered. This state also shares a border with Mexico, so we have many Latin American refugees staying with us. I headed out there four years ago to set up the Center for Action and Contemplation. There we try to educate people in a spirituality of social justice.

The city of Albuquerque lies in the middle of the desert and is surrounded by many Indian tribes. That's why it's a wonderful place if you're on a quest for wisdom. But it looks as if wherever you find positive spiritual energy you also find negative spiritual energy. The place where the Indians have prayed for centuries is the place where we've created the instruments of death. And Christians have to go to precisely this place to reflect on the meaning of the Gospel and to discover what light and darkness, good and evil, are.

A talk given in the Peace Church, Darmstadt, March 20, 1990.

This evening's topic deals with what Jesus said about the simple life. Just this once I would like to tackle this subject in a completely different way. Of course, we could always go through the familiar texts from Luke, Mark, and the Acts of the Apostles, one after the other, where Jesus quite clearly says that we should live simply and poorly in this world. But then it would look as if the point was simply to convince or inspire people to do what's right. And after twenty years as a preacher I've noticed that sermons and inspirational work in themselves have no long-term effect. We have to find the truth, *really* find it and believe in it *for its own sake*.

All too long we've tried to motivate people through guilt feelings or fear. We've said, "You have to do this or that, otherwise God won't love you." And if we do the thing in question, then we *really* don't do it. Because heart, head, and gut don't agree, but are at war with one another.

So let's take a completely different tack today. How is it that after two thousand years of meditation on Jesus Christ we've managed so effectively to avoid everything that he taught so unequivocally? This is true of all the churches. *All* of us, for example, have evaded the Sermon on the Mount. *All* of us have evaded the unmistakable teaching of Jesus' teaching on poverty. *All* of us have evaded Jesus' clear directive on non-violence. *All* of us have evaded his straightforward doctrine of loving your enemies.

Jesus is too much for us. The Church is a kind of collective teenager. In our maturation process as a Christian Church we've grown about a year per century; this means we'll soon be twenty. Perhaps we're gradually getting ready to let the Gospel talk turkey to us. We always wanted to have answers, because in an early stage of life the first thing we need is certainty. But Jesus doesn't offer us any certainties; he offers us a journey of faith. Jesus doesn't give us many answers; he tells us what the right questions are, what questions the human soul has to wrestle with to stumble onto Christ and *the* truth.

Our formulations determine what we're really looking for. Our questions determine what we ultimately find and discover. Answers acquire power too quickly; they often turn our words into ammunition to be used against others. And answers make trust unnecessary, they make listening dispensable, they make relations with others superfluous. I don't need *you* to take my journey. I need only my head, my certainties, and my conclusions. It's all private. But Jesus said we have to live in this world so as to be dependent on one another. That means the real meaning of a poor life is a life of radical dependency, so that I can't arrange my life in such a way that I don't need you. We can't do it alone.

We have to avoid several things here: Don't trivialize the words of Jesus by asking, for example: "Does he really want that from me?" So let's not reach too hastily for an answer instead of letting ourselves be invited to a process. Don't generalize too early by asking, for example, "Where would we be if we all did this or that?" That way we often create grotesque scenarios and stifle Jesus' real demand on us. For example, when we discuss Jesus' teaching on non-violence, people say: "Do you mean to tell me that if someone comes into my house with a gun and wants to kill my wife and my children, I shouldn't defend myself?"

At least one reason for this lies in the fact that until now the Gospel has been expounded by a small elite group. I would have to describe this group as mostly made up of men, educated men, Europeans and later North Americans. There's no objection to be made per se against these people — I'm one of them myself. But we've had a monopoly for too long. And in this world there is still a whole mass of other people who have a whole mass of other insights. The white man first raises the questions of power and control. The questions that we pose to the Gospel are always questions that come out of this bias. That's why we just can't hear questions like the one about poverty. We can't hear the question about non-violence. Because Christians have needed good excuses to get permission to kill one another. The question about loving one's enemy can't be heard.

But in our time something wonderful is happening. For the first time in its history the Church is becoming truly universal. This means that the Gospel is being reread and rediscovered by altogether different eyes. In the process altogether different questions are being raised. And because the new readers are approaching the Gospel with completely new formulations of the issues, we also notice that they wind up with completely different answers. And even we white men say, "How come we never saw that?"

This evening I would like to give at least one example of this and speak about a text from the nineteenth chapter of Luke, the parable of the pounds. I could never stand this story, because I went to Catholic school in America and on the first day of school the priest gave a sermon on it, admonishing us to be good, hard-working pupils and get As and Bs but no Cs. We were supposed to be like the first and the second man in the parable, not like the third. That's why it always rubbed me the wrong way. I would now like to read the story to you and see whether there might not be a completely different approach to it.

The interpretation that I'll present comes from a base community in Latin America, made up of quite simple and uneducated people, who don't consider themselves theological scholars. But these interpretations have come to

America and are now being taken over by some of the best theologians. Many of them are convinced that we have finally discovered the true meaning of this text.

"He proceeded to tell them a parable, because he was near to Jerusalem, and because they supposed that the kingdom of God was to appear immediately." This is the starting point. These people expect that a simple, unproblematic shift of power is just about to occur. And Jesus tells himself: I have an urgent need to talk to these people. I believe they have no idea what price they'll have to pay. I believe they don't know what God's Kingdom costs.

"He said therefore, 'A nobleman went into a far country to receive a kingdom.'" Like all good preachers, he starts off with a memorable political event, so that every listener knows what he's talking about. We think, of course, that when Jesus mentions the word "king," he means God the Father. But in reality this refers to Archelaos, the son of Herod. Back then everyone knew that Herod's son had gone on a three-year furlough to Rome after becoming king.

Before heading off, Jesus' "nobleman" has ten of his servants summoned and gives each of them ten pounds. "Trade with these till I come." The historical situation behind this is that before he went to Rome, Archelaos appointed viceroys. And he expected these men to collect the same unfair taxes that he had. He wanted them to oppress the poor the same way he had. When he got back, of course, he wanted to rake in the whole profit. Furthermore it's a historical fact that a delegation of the country's inhabitants was sent after him to Rome with the message, "Don't come back; stay where you are." This is exactly what the next verse says: "But his citizens hated him and sent an embassy after him, saying, 'We do not want this man to reign over us.'"

Thus Jesus isn't talking about some sort of rejection of God and God's gifts, but about altogether down-to-earth topics of politics and oppression. The story proceeds: "When he returned, having received the kingdom, he commanded these servants, to whom he had given the money, to be called to him, that he might know what they had gained by trading. The first came before him, saying, 'Lord, your pound has made ten pounds more.'" So this viceroy was just the same sort of cutthroat as Archelaos himself. "And he said to him, 'Well done, good servant. Because you have been faithful in very little, you shall have authority over ten cities.'" What Jesus is saying to his disciples is, "If you play along with their game, they'll reward you for it. The world takes care of its own."

"And the second came, saying, 'Lord, your pound has made five pounds.' And he said to him, 'And you are to be over five cities.'" I used to think that the first two servants were the heroes; but that's a prejudice of the capitalist mind-set. In reality the first two are blackguards, and the third is the hero. "Then another came, saying, 'Lord, here is your pound, which I kept laid away in a napkin; for I was afraid of you, because you are a severe man; you take up what you did not lay down'" — this is precisely the judgment that Jesus passes on the world — "'and reap what you did not sow.'" Ronald Reagan called this the "trickle-down effect." He claimed that by some obscure miracle the poor would get richer as soon as the rich got still richer. This is a very comfortable myth for the people who are right up there on top.

"He said to him, 'I will condemn you out of your own mouth, you wicked servant! You knew that I was a severe man, taking up what I did not lay down and reaping what I did not sow. Why then did you not put my money into the bank, and at my coming I should have collected it with interest?' " The third man is the one who is really prepared to take the consequences of his inner obedience. Nowadays we would call this "civil disobedience." We would say: He's responding to a deeper truth; and this *deeper* truth always leads us into conflict with the *superficial* truth. "And he said to those who stood by, 'Take the pound from him, and give it to him who has the ten pounds.' "

But now we suddenly hear a hesitant voice from the wings saying, "Lord, he has ten pounds." Why should the rich always get richer, and the poor always get poorer? The world takes care of its own. But Jesus taught his disciples not to play along with this system. This is the last parable in the Gospel of Luke, which Jesus tells before he enters Jerusalem to be *crucified*. If you want to live the truth, then you must be prepared to pay the price for it. Sometimes it seems that Jesus' only program for social reform is *non-cooperation* and *non-idolatry*, which will usually necessitate living a simple life.

In the first three centuries of church history the Gospel spoke primarily (though not exclusively) to those who belonged to the lower classes, not to the middle and upper classes. It was always the little people who trusted it and the people on top who fought it. But in the year 313 Emperor Constantine did us a "great favor." He declared Christianity an established religion in the Roman empire. Overnight we changed, so to speak, from underdogs to top dogs.

In the fifth century St. Hilarion wrote:

Instead, today we fight a more dangerous persecutor, an enemy who flatters us, namely the mighty Roman emperor. He no longer wounds our backs, he bedecks our chests with medals. He doesn't confiscate our goods; on the contrary, he gives us gifts. He doesn't force us to be really free by locking us up; he sends us into slavery by honoring us in his palace. He doesn't attack us with his resources, but he takes possession of our hearts. He doesn't hack our heads off with the sword, but he kills our spirit with gold. He doesn't officially threaten us with the stake, but he secretly kindles the fire of hell. He doesn't wage any battles against us, but he adores our Christ, so that he can reign unhindered. He confirms Christ so as to deny him in reality. He proclaims unity, but he prevents communion.

We should try to win back our lower place. Jesus says that he has come to preach the Gospel to the poor since in fact they're the only ones who can hear it! They don't have to prove or protect anything. We always have to ask: In what sense are we ourselves rich? What do we have to defend? What principles do we have to prove? What keeps us from being open and poor? The issue isn't primarily material goods, but our spiritual and intellectual goods, my ego, my reputation, my self-image, my need to be right, my need to be successful, my need to have everything under control, my need to be loved. These are the capital sins that we try to describe in *Discovering the Enneagram*.

The words of the Gospel never let us live in self-satisfaction. Rather they always make us empty. They always make us repeat the truth of Mary's "Let it be done to me according to *your* word." They allow us to keep our wounds open so we can receive Christ in us. It seems we're quite incapable of welcoming Christ, because we're so stuffed full of ourselves. The real thing we have to let go of is our self. We aren't really free until we're free from ourselves.

The subject of the last eight cassette tapes that I recorded in America, "A Spirituality of Subtraction," goes back to the German mystic Meister Eckhart. Meister Eckhart said that the spiritual life has more to do with subtraction than with addition. But in the capitalistic West here's what we've done with the Gospel: We keep climbing high up the ladder of spiritual success, and we've turned the Gospel into a matter of addition instead of subtraction. All we can do is get ourselves out of the way! Then God will be evident. Then we can easily welcome Christ. We've been allowed to take ourselves so seriously, although we're only a tiny moment of consciousness. I'm just a tiny part of creation, a particle that reflects only a fragment of God's glory. And yet that's enough.

It's really that simple. But if we haven't lived and experienced enough within ourselves, we're tempted to accumulate more and more outer things as substitutes for self-worth. This, of course, is the great spiritual illusion. We needn't acquire what we already have.

My second great spiritual teacher, after Jesus, was Francis of Assisi. He spent his whole life so that he could become smaller, to go down and become a "brother of the lower class." He told us that we should always live at the bottom, since only there can we really experience the truth. But this truth is hard to grasp in a world that says, "Life takes place in the center, and not on the periphery."

You need a great deal of faith to believe that there's enough on the margin too. And nevertheless that's really been my experience. I had the privilege of visiting many countries in the Third World. There I always found that the poor of this world are often much happier than most of us. They don't need to constantly project their soul onto things, and so they can find it within themselves. They can't work from the assumption that external things will offer them fulfillment. A woman from the Philippines once told me: "Father, we have nothing except God and our community." I believe that's the only thing the Gospel promises us. It offers us a way that leads to God and a way that leads to one another.

But we want security, although the Gospel never promised us security in this world. Jesus also never said that we had a responsibility to make the world secure. Instead he said that we should do the truth. Since the beginning of time every person who comes into the world is born into insecurity. We can't really protect ourselves against this insecurity, which belongs to our humanness, without also ultimately blocking ourselves off from God. Because the truth can reach us only when we find ourselves at a place of dependency, openness, "longing and thirsting."

We men, who are on top, are actually at the very bottom of the trap. At first glance we look like the system's winners, but in reality we're its victims. We're much less free than most women. In America we observe that the women are about fifteen years ahead of us in their development, because they're not so tangled in the lies of the system and not so stuck in the trap of competition and achievement. That's why they have more freedom to trust a deeper wisdom — unless they're joining in the same male system, which many now are.

It's amazing: Christianity is the only religion that dares to call God a *lamb*. And nevertheless we've spent two thousand years avoiding vulnerability. Paul says straight out, "When I am weak, I am strong" (2 Cor. 12:10). But we're afraid of discovering this sort of strength. We haven't ever been there, and so we don't know whether it's really strength. And yet it's the only kind of power that the Gospel offers us. The world will never understand this kind of power; but we have to understand it, if we really want to be the Church and if the Church wants to have any kind of credibility.

Karl Rahner, who preached from this very pulpit, once said: If by the next century we don't rediscover the mystical roots of Christianity and the connection between the mystical and the political, then we can forget all about Christianity. Because then Christianity is part of the problem rather than part of the solution.

Spirituality and faith have more to do with subtraction, with becoming *less*, than with addition, with becoming *more*. First we have to let go of the *past:* We all carry large packages of guilt around with us. It's clear to all of us what we *didn't* do and what we did *wrong*. But even our guilt feelings can turn into an ego trip. I dragged guilt feelings around with me so long as I had the need to consider myself especially valuable. When I finally let go of the need to feel "worthy," I noticed that my guilt feelings were just one long circling around myself. That means most of my guilt feelings just served my own ends. I can easily talk myself into guilt feelings over trifles so that I don't have to tackle the really important things.

I think that before they go into the city Jesus is trying to tell the disciples: There are very big things at stake here, not the hothouse virtues that middle-class Christianity worries over. That kind of Christianity is too privatized, too individualistic, and basically too unimportant, because we're constantly engaged in contemplating our navels and never meet Christ. We always meet a new version of ourselves and live in a vicious circle of useless guilt feelings.

But the point isn't just to let go of the past; it's to let go of the *future* too. We have to let go of fear of the future, of our cares and our exaggerated need for security. Finally we also have to let go of the *present*, the need to be something special here and now. If I have too great a need to be loved, if I say all this here so that you'll applaud afterward, then I'm not free and I'm also not saying the full truth, but only a little truth.

One of the hardest things to do in letting go is giving up the need to be something. The more positive our self-image, the more dangerous it is. The more pious it is, the more dangerous it is. And the most dangerous thing of all is to be a professional Christian. That's why it's always the Pharisees and scribes who kill Jesus, because they have to defend their theology — and in this theology there's no place for the reality of an incarnate Christ. If we're honest, we probably find it a bit disappointing that Jesus Christ came as a completely normal human being.

Letting go of the present means giving up our self-image, our titles, our public image. I think this is one of the many meanings of the First Commandment: "You shall have no other gods before me." What's at stake here are not just false images of God (which mostly serve our purposes), but also comfortable images of ourselves. That's probably what the saints meant when they said: We have to move to the place of faith, to the place of self-forgetfulness, of nothingness.

When C. G. Jung was an old man, one of his disciples read John Bunyan's *Pilgrim's Progress*; and he asked Jung, "What has your pilgrimage really been?" And Jung answered: "My journey consisted in climbing down ten thousand ladders so that now at the end of my life I can extend the hand of friendship to this little clod of earth that I am." That's a free man. The word "human" comes from the Latin *humus*, which means earth. Being human means acknowledging that we're made from the earth and will return to the earth. For a few years we dance around on the stage of life and have the chance to reflect a little bit of God's glory. We are earth that has come to consciousness. If we discover this power in ourselves and know that we are God's creatures, that we come from God and return to God, that's enough. You can't grasp this with logic; even this sermon won't convince anyone that this is how it is. You have to experience it yourself, by going on the journey yourself and walking the path yourself. That's why we call our center in New Mexico the Center for Action and Contemplation, because only when we come to the contemplative vision within do we find the real basis of the Gospel.

This is exactly what Jesus does in the forty days in the wilderness: He goes to a place of emptiness. And it says: He fasted for forty days, meaning, he made himself empty. He stared down the demon who told him, "You have to be successful." And he answered, "No, I don't need that." When he stood on the pinnacle of the temple, he stared down the second who told him, "You have to be on the right religious track." This demon could quote Scripture! And Jesus said: "Get lost. I don't need this game." Finally he met the demon who told him, "You can do the will of God with the tools of power." But the price of power is falling down before Satan.

We all have to start from the assumption that our path too leads into the wilderness and that we have to look exactly the same three demons in the eye: the need to be successful, the need to be righteous or religious, and the need to have power and get everything under control. Until we have stared down these three demons within us, there is no possibility of getting out of the wilderness and proclaiming the Kingdom of God. Otherwise we'll always be proclaiming our own kingdom. We use the Gospel to enthrone ourselves, and then the inner and the outer ways split apart. God calls all of you to take the path of the inner truth — and that means taking responsibility for *everything* that's in you: for what pleases you and for what you're ashamed of, for the rich person inside you and for the poor one. Francis of Assisi called this, "loving the leper within us." If you learn to love the poor one within you, you'll discover that you have room to have compassion "outside" too, that there's room in you for others, for those who are different from you, for the least among your brothers and sisters.

Less really *is* more. Only those who have nothing to prove and nothing to protect, those who have in them a broad space big enough to embrace every part of their own soul, can receive the Christ. And Christ himself will lead us on this path.

QUESTIONS and ANSWERS

Q. *Nothing gets done by throwing demands in people's faces. Could you once again tell us how you're trying now to reach people without rigid orders or demands?*

A. First, of course, I'd like to preach the great vision of the Reign of God. Then in this context I'd like to pass along to others an authentic process of hearing. Here the content is not as important as that the process itself gets launched. It's a new way you can listen to God. The process is designed so that in the end the conclusions you draw will really be your own and not mine, the conclusions I've grafted onto you. You have to believe the Gospel for yourself. We learn in this process not to take ourselves too seriously, to put ourselves aside, to pull back. And I believe all great spiritual exercises aim at achieving the same thing. Why does Jesus teach us, for example, to love our enemies? So that they'll become Christians? Perhaps — that would be fine, of course — but he probably says it mainly so that *we* meet those *we* are afraid of, and thus *we* can be liberated from our fear. Many people who have entered missionary service have been converted by the people they went to convert.

And that's why the statement holds that we have to be ready to find Christ where we didn't expect him before. In Matthew 25, the only description of the Last Judgment that we have, we don't meet anybody with a clearly defined theology. But we do find people who have learned to see and hear and pull back. Then you can grab God with both hands, so to speak. In his discourse on the Last Judgment Jesus says that we'll be judged simply on whether we were able to recognize Christ in the least of our brothers and sisters. We won't be judged by the Ten Commandments nor by whether we recognized Christ in other members of our denomination, but perhaps in people who are completely different from us. This is the most radical form of conversion I can imagine. I'll say it again: This is a question of seeing. I believe, therefore, that the Gospel imparts to us in the first instance a process and not a specific series of propositions about faith. If we turn the Gospel into a series of dogmas, we'll spend our whole life defending them. And think about this: We don't possess our possessions; in the final analysis they possess us. That holds for our theological possessions too.

Q. *How do you live, in very practical terms? For example, how do you deal with money? How do the people in the Center for Action and Contemplation handle these goals?*

In "New Jerusalem" we didn't have a full community of goods. We came to the conclusion that it would create more problems than it would solve. But the people in my community had many other creative possibilities of supporting one another, because our life was shared on a very deep level, and we trusted one another. Mothers share child care and give one another free time. Men share tools and help in house repair. They all helped refugees.

In New Mexico we're not an actual "symbiotic" community. This time I'm trying to do things differently. In Cincinnati we built a self-conscious community that calls itself "New Jerusalem." We spent an enormous amount of energy developing the art of community. From that, many people got a vision of the Reign of God and how they could serve the world. But there's still another way to achieve the same thing: to call men and women together who already have a common vision of justice and mission. I'm convinced that community will then appear as a *by-product*, so to speak. But it is not an end in itself.

Today, after four years, I also think this is the better method for our current situation. The topics of concern today are much too big and too problematic: refugees, the homeless, prison reform, nuclear disarmament. When the topics of the Gospel become so real, then we simply know that we need the Body of Christ to discover with one another what's at stake and also how to deal with one another. Perhaps we've watered down the Gospel so much because we only took individuals as our starting point. I don't think I've been very practical for you, but I hope this gives you the context out of which practical decisions will emerge.

Q. *You've spoken about a life in poverty and powerlessness. What do you think about technological progress? Do you see a danger in it? Do you see dangers in scientific research? Should the limits of what's permitted to human beings be set earlier or later?*

A. Centuries ago we forgot how to have a genuine dialogue with technology, and so technology has gone on developing, but not our wisdom. We've divided the world up quite comfortably into religion on the one side and secular things on the other. As a Church we've lost the capacity to hold an authentic dialogue with the world; and we've withdrawn to our closed Christian world, because we're only capable of talking with people who were already of our opinion anyway. That's why money has the primary say these days, because we've stopped saying anything to money. Technology has the floor, because we never said a word to technology. This is a vocation that many of you have. Please don't spend the rest of your lives in churches. Use the experience that you've had of the truth and of the Word of God to de-idolize the systems of this world. Use this experience to raise critical questions from the standpoint of your faith. Jesus taught us that we should love people and use things. But you and I live in countries that use people and love things. And this reversal has occurred because we didn't manage to reconcile our faith and the world.

Every Friday morning in the neighborhood of our center we hold a prayer vigil in front of the gates of a nuclear laboratory. We don't point the finger threateningly at the people

who work there. We hold posters up that raise questions of
faith. In the beginning we got a lot of angry gestures and
cries of rage. But after three months the situation changed.
They had learned in the meantime that we weren't their
enemies; they sensed we were posing intelligent religious
questions out of concern for the world — as brothers and
sisters. Last Ash Wednesday they even invited me into the
barracks to celebrate Mass there. And some people said:
"That guy you're inviting in here is our enemy." But the
church was full, and after the service the people stayed an
extra hour to talk with me. Now we have a dialogue every
month, and I myself can scarcely believe how far we've
gotten on this way with one another.

We do not call the people who work there evil. We know
that as individuals they're as good as we are and perhaps
even better. I still believe that they're participating in something that on the whole and as a system is evil, but as
individuals they're good. As Christians we've too long neglected to establish a link between individual and structural
sin. We've been busy the whole time denouncing *individual*
sin. But it's the *institutionalized* sin that's chiefly responsible
for the world's injustice.

Sometimes there are simple people who are wiser than
we are. There's another nuclear laboratory in New Mexico, at Los Alamos, where the atomic bomb was invented.
Around this region three Catholic Indian tribes are settled.
Among the tribes the Catholics are mixed in with those
who adhere to their traditional religion. Five years ago as
our bishops were debating whether we should condemn
the doctrine of deterrence as morally bad from the Christian point of view, the Indians began quietly to perform an
"exorcism" over Los Alamos. With their so-called primitive
wisdom they have no doubt that this is the place where

the destruction of the world is being prepared. You have to wonder where the real wisdom lies. Our Christ is so great that we know he has no fear of he truth. Hence as Christians we have to be people who have the freedom to integrate psychology, history and theology, anthropology and sociology: we needn't be afraid of anything.

As soon as we've found our center, we no longer have to defend our boundaries. We've spent so many years defending our boundaries because we weren't sure of our center. I personally believe that only contemplative prayer can lead us to our center. So I'll give you a piece of advice that may strike you as peculiar: I encourage you to enter upon a radical inner path of prayer. The place in you that seems to be the most intimate is in reality the most universal and worldwide. At this place you'll find the freedom to confront science and technology and connect them with faith and morality.

Q. *What is your vision of a future world? Could New Jerusalem be a place where different religions meet without fear, listen to and learn from each other? Could we learn something from other religions?*

A. Twenty-five years ago at the Second Vatican Council the bishops composed some wonderful documents. Unfortunately the Church for the most part didn't take them very seriously. One of these documents was about the non-Christian religions. It says: We have no doubt that Christ is for us *the* Word of God. Christ is the one who most fully reveals the heart of the Father. As a matter of fact nobody else does claim to be the Son of God. But this doesn't mean that the other religions can't also be the "words" of God. If we have our firmly based foundation, then we need not fear the other words of God, and we don't have to worry that we're losing our own center.

I admit that you already have to be very mature to get to this point. You can't begin here. It might sound strange, but I always emphasize that you have to start conservative. You have to begin somewhere and send down deep roots at one place. We have to go the whole way with Christ and only then will we meet the cosmic Christ. Then we will no longer need to defend our frontiers so stubbornly, and we can see that truth can be found in the other great world religions too. I know that many people are not ready for this yet, and I have to admit that I myself took a very long time to get to this point. But why else would Jesus say so often, Don't be afraid, don't be afraid! A large percentage of Christians are still afraid: as if God needed us to defend divine truth, as if God needed us to defend God's work. I believe that in reality we don't at all love the Christ who is the Alpha and Omega of history; instead we love a little Jesus whom we can stick in our pocket.

Q. *On this path what is the meaning of the spiritual gifts, charisms, signs and wonders, the transcendent?*

A. As soon as we distance ourselves from the control center of our brains, as soon as we free ourselves from the comfortable principles of our preconceived theology. (I'm not saying that theology is something bad; we need good theology and reflection.) But as soon as we've gotten to the point where you know only "Actually I know nothing," then the transcendent can reach us. Then you're no longer caught in the myth of reason, the myth of science. Then you're open to the non-rational as well, to grace, to the transcendent, to the burning bush. It's all a matter of seeing.

I believe that God often comes into this world quite unexpectedly, uninvited, and even unwanted. Take the charisms, for example, the many spiritual gifts of healing, tongues, and forgiveness; through them we experience the immediate action of God in this world. They're necessary, so that we can develop a taste for the holy. It's very sad that in Western Christianity so few people have a genuine sense of the sacred or an authentic access to it, the feeling that "I'd just like to kneel down." Without this sense of the sacred religion very quickly becomes sterile and rigid.

But on the other hand we can't immediately strive for transcendental or emotional experiences of faith, because if we do they can easily become a cheap substitute for real faith. Faith is ultimately faith, which means to believe and to know — *without* experience and *without* feelings. We might have to spend a whole lifetime walking in darkness, recalling the little we've experienced in the light. I'll just take the most familiar and widespread charism, "speaking in tongues." It's the least of the spiritual gifts and nevertheless a very important one. Because when we speak in tongues then we have to abandon our need for control and our constant need to explain everything. We have to drop the predominance of reason.

There are many indications that praying the rosary became customary in the Catholic Church when speaking in tongues had died out. Moving the fingers with the beads has the same effect: We stop having to understand everything; we simply sit in the presence of the mystery and say, "Ah." Some of the Indians in our region have learned contemplative prayer without calling it that. When they get up in the morning, their mother tells them: "Don't say anything, go to the door that opens to the east. Stand there and look at the rising sun, and just make a slow gesture of welcome." That doesn't sound especially sublime. But I believe it's precisely because of such quiet simple gestures that these people have a sense for the holy. They're ready for God to enter their world. When we lose this openness to the transcendent, then we probably lose contact with the God who is really God.

Q. *You said that faith calls for not just a letting go of rational thinking, but even of feelings and emotions. How do you mean that?*

A. I didn't say you should forbid yourself emotions or cut off the feelings; but you should not deliberately aim for emotions. We experience a purification through trials, so that we can be freed from our attachment to feelings and not take the transitory emotions too seriously. We have to let go of them, so that really great emotions can come to light, genuine passions that free us for leading a completely different life. That's why emotions have an important function in the spiritual life, but we shouldn't become dependent on them. And we should not strive for them for their own sake.

Normally it goes like this: The more we grow in faith, the fewer emotional experiences we'll have. Teresa of Avila, who has written such wonderful things about the dark night of purification, says that she spent eighteen years without one comforting emotion. But afterward she experienced quite deep ecstatic feeling. Many of us are so emotionally overstimulated (we watch too many movies, we hear too much music) that we're no longer capable of the really great feelings. We're not prepared for the feelings that really convert and change us. That is why some sort of "fasting" experience is so important for us. That's the meaning and the original significance of the forty days of Lent.

Q. *You said that we shouldn't be so heavily dependent on the recognition of other people. How can we develop a healthy feeling of self-worth?*

A. We can't consciously decide to have a positive self-image. I'd like to say that it happens to us, it "befalls" us. As Christians we can't save ourselves; we get saved. If we go to too much trouble fishing for compliments, say, then we don't believe the compliments when we get them. The only gifts that heal us are the ones that are voluntarily given. If we play a game where we have to kiss our girlfriend, then the kiss doesn't feel half as good as the kiss she gives us of her own free will. The most important thing we need is a spiritual conversion so that I no longer have to defend my negative *or* my positive image.

What we need here is not excessive self-consciousness, but authentic contemplation. When we discover ourselves "hidden with Christ in God," we don't *need* any kind of self-image at all. I hope this doesn't sound too esoteric. Because it isn't; it's what happens in true prayer. This is what will happen when we expose ourselves to silence and stop exposing ourselves to the judgments of the world, when we don't continuously "pick up" the energy of others and don't always have to think about what others think of us and what they take us to be. We are who we are in God — no more and no less.

That's why I have to go into the wilderness, where I let God call me by name, to a deeper place. This is the peace that the world can't give. But I promise you that it's also the peace that the world can no longer take from you. This peace doesn't come about because we do anything right or wrong. The point is, we have to discover what we have always been in God. When we get to this place, we will know and love ourselves, and that in spite of all the negative and opposing evidence. It is the spacious place of the soul. To live there is finally to be at home. The soul can't be fixed. It just is. This first and final home we carry with us all our lives. God is also at home there, and when we return we have discovered simplicity.